THE FIGHT OF MY LIFE

LIVING WITH CYSTIC FIBROSIS
AND SURVIVING MY DOUBLE LUNG TRANSPLANT

William D. Mahaney III

On the Cover:
Photo of me at three years old

Copyright © 2012 William Mahaney
All rights reserved.
ISBN: 1470136570
ISBN-13: 978-1470136574

This story is dedicated
to my daughter, Mikaela Fay,
our wonderful, beautiful miracle

"It is supposed that Cystic Fibrosis appeared about 3,000 BC as a cause of migration of peoples, gene mutations, and new conditions in nourishment. Although the entire clinical spectrum of CF was not recognized until the 1930s, certain aspects of CF were identified much earlier. Indeed, literature from Germany and Switzerland in the 18th century warned *Wehe dem Kind, das beim Kuß auf die Stirn salzig schmekt, er ist verhext und muss bald sterbe* or "Woe to the child who tastes salty from a kiss on the brow, for he is cursed and soon must die," recognizing the association between the salt loss in CF and illness."[9]

Just the Facts

There are 6,000 genetic health conditions with which an individual could potentially be born. If you're fortunate you are born with none of them. A baby can enter into this world with Down Syndrome, Sickle Cell Anemia or Cystic Fibrosis to name just a few of many. Perhaps you have heard of the three I just listed. Maybe you recognize only one or two.

There are approximately 7 million people alive today with Down Syndrome. A quarter of a million babies are born each year with Sickle Cell Anemia, mostly in Africa. Approximately 70,000 individuals worldwide live with Cystic Fibrosis.

Seventy thousand people worldwide doesn't seem like a lot compared to 7 million. After all, seventy thousand people would only fill an average National Football League stadium. If you're like most people you're probably thinking, "Now what exactly is cystic fibrosis"? You're almost positive you've heard of it and you know having cystic fibrosis is certainly not a good thing, but you really don't know anything more about the illness than that. Certainly you're aware of diabetes, cancer, AIDS and heart disease. So what is cystic fibrosis? Who gets it, why do you get it, how serious is it and how common is it?

Well, like most diseases or illnesses, cystic fibrosis is complicated. I may not be able to answer all the questions about cystic fibrosis, but what I can tell you is what it's like having cystic fibrosis (CF), because this is the story of my life with it.

What is cys·tic fi·bro·sis ?
[sìstik fī brŏssiss]

Here is a well defined, simple explanation of cystic fibrosis. It gives the average person a good understanding of the disease.

"CF is caused by a mutation in the gene for the protein cystic fibrosis transmembrane conductance regulator (CFTR). This protein is required to regulate the components of sweat, digestive juices, and mucus. Cystic fibrosis affects the body's ability to move salt and water in and out of cells. This defect causes the lungs and pancreas to secrete abnormally thick mucus that blocks passageways and prevents proper function. It primarily affects the lungs, digestive system and pancreas."[9]

"CF affects approximately 30,000 children and young adults in the United States and 70,000 people worldwide. Each year, about 1,000 babies are born with CF.
CF primarily affects people of white northern-European descent (1 in 3,200). Rates are much lower in Hispanic (1 in 9,200), African-American (1 in 15,000) and Asian (1 in 31,000) populations.

Most children with CF are diagnosed by age two, and now many symptoms of CF can be treated with drugs and nutritional supplements. Close attention to and prompt treatment of respiratory and digestive complications have dramatically increased the expected life span of a person with CF. While in the 1950s, children with CF rarely lived past age 6, today about half of all people with CF live past age 37, with the median life span expected to increase as treatments are improved."[13]

You are born with cystic fibrosis. You cannot catch it or give it to someone, like a cold.

Don't Bet These Odds

I know both my parents felt an extreme sense of guilt that I had been born with such a terrible disease. It took some time for the doctors to come to a conclusion on what exactly I had, but when the final diagnosis was disclosed, I can only imagine what was going through their heads. I would think they wished there was something they could have done to prevent this from happening or perhaps hoped that there was something to make it go away. But of course neither of them could have known or prevented my fate, and there is medically nothing that can be done to make CF go away.

So what were the odds of me getting this disease while both my sisters did not. Well, that's about a 25% chance, and this is how it happens…

"Each of us has 23 pairs of chromosomes. Each chromosome pair contains the same genes, but not necessarily the same gene code. For instance, both chromosomes in the pair that determines hair color will contain a color gene, but one may be brown and the other one blonde. Cystic fibrosis (CF) is caused by a mutation of the cystic fibrosis transmembrane regulator (CFTR) gene.

If you are a CF carrier, it means that one of your CFTR genes is normal, and the other contains a mutation that is known to cause cystic fibrosis. Your child will inherit one chromosome of each pair from you, and one from your partner. If your child gets the chromosome containing the mutated CFTR gene from both of you, they will have two mutated copies. Thus, your child will have CF. If they inherit a mutated chromosome from one of you and a normal one from the other, they will be a CF carrier, will not have CF but could pass the disease to their child.

Broken down into odds, if the parents are both carriers, your child has a 25% chance of having CF, a 50% chance of being a carrier, and a 25% chance of neither having nor carrying CF.

If your partner is not a CF carrier, it will be impossible for your child to have CF because he can only inherit normal copies of the CFTR gene from your partner. However, your child will have a 25% chance of being a carrier, which would occur if he received the mutated CFTR gene from you. Meaning he could pass it on to his children."[1]

Confused enough yet? Chromosomes (humans have 23 pairs of chromosomes, for a total of 46) and genes (25,000 of them in our body) effect who we are and what we are, and although researchers do not know what function all our genes perform, what is known that you *don't* want to be born with two CFTR muted genes. Then you will be born with cystic fibrosis.

As you will read, we cystics are small in number, only 70,000, give or take but we are big in the will to fight. And it's really all about the fight, both physical and emotional, because having cystic fibrosis really is the fight of your life.

The Start of a New Beginning
November 19, 2009

I heard my wife's voice, my moms, my sisters, nothing.
Are you in pain? I shook my head no.
Are you in any pain? I shook my head no.
Are you in pain? No.

I remember being asked this at least 3 times, then I remember someone telling me they were going to take out my trachea tube. I remember the feeling of it being pulled out my throat, my mouth, then I was breathing on my own, an important step. I was vaguely aware of the sensation of taking in the breaths, in, out, in, out and no trachea tube being put back down my throat, I was warned it could be reinserted if it was necessary,
then nothing.

I was asked my name, where I was, why I was there and what year it was. These questions determined if I had experienced any brain damage. I was able to answer them correctly, I think,
and then nothing.

My first three or four days were a blur, the morphine made me confused, disoriented unable to focus or speak clearly. I always believed that I was sitting at the foot of my bed. I was so close I could have fallen off the end, but nobody seemed concerned. I told my family over and over that I could not speak clearly with them, the words would not come out, they weren't making sense and I felt like I had a stroke. They seemed to have no reaction, like they weren't even listening. I tested all my limbs, none were immobile, yet the sensation of having one was definite. Was it all the heavy medication I was on, doing crazy things to my mind, crazy things to my brain...
and then nothing.

After first hearing my families voices I was no longer aware of their coming or going or when my wife Deb was there, although she has since told me she was there daily, almost all day, each day, daily,
then nothing.

I don't remember having the morphine available to me with the squeeze of a button, but I did and apparently I used it. I did not like it,
then nothing.

After many blurred days went by it was decided I was to be given an epidural and Percocet in place of the morphine. This helped and I was able to at least form complete thoughts and sentences.
I was finally starting to become ….something.

A Problem of Unknown Proportions
May 16, 1957

I was born on May 16th, 1957 in Buffalo, NY. The baby boom generation (1946-1964) was nearing its' end. Buffalo in the late 1950's was a happenin' place to live. The city and suburbs were growing. Elvis Presley had come to town in April, just a month before I was born. The area was prosperous, employment was good. Steel and grain were the major industries that kept the wheels of prosperity turning.

Buffalo was known as a major metropolitan area in 1957 and was the 20th largest city in the United States with a population of approximately 500,000. In 1957 Buffalo didn't have the reputation as a snow city like it does today. It did have one big-ass crippling snow storm in 1977 that made international news and since then it's been branded the snow capital of the world. Yes, it snows here in Buffalo, but Syracuse, NY just a two hour drive down the New York State Thruway gets more snow annually than Buffalo. Buffalo is very similar to almost any city within a 200 mile radius in regards to overall climate. That includes places like Cleveland, OH, Allentown, PA or Toronto, Canada.

The area of Buffalo my family lived in is the small suburban village of Depew. My family included my mom and dad and my two older sisters, Candy and Holly, although now they prefer the professionalism of Candace and Hollis, which I never call them. My mom was a housewife by the time I was born, but before that she took classes in interior decorating. My father was slowly working his way up the professional ladder as a certified public accountant.

I think my mother always knew there was something not quite right with her baby Billy(that's me). After my birth a nurse that was caring for me handed me over to my mother and said that she noticed a large amount of phlegm when she suctioned me out. My mom discounted the comment, but never forgot it.

Although I was born a seemingly normal, healthy baby boy her mother's intuition told her otherwise. My mom already had two healthy children so she thought she knew what to expect from me. She was prepared for the stinky, mealy bowel movements all babies have, but mine were definitely not like those. Greasy, wet and smelly was an understatement. My butt used to sting from the constant diarrhea I had and I was having many, many more BM's than a baby and then toddler should be having. I seemed to be a normal child on the outside, amazingly stinky on the inside.

Me on my toy tractor in 1962. I'm 5 years old

I remember always being "uncomfortable" but believed this is how I was supposed to be. I spent a lot of time in the bathroom on the toilet but I was used to that and it became was just another component of my childhood. In my post diaper years I can't even begin to tell you how many times I can recall my mom helping me out of my soiled pants, cleaning my burning from the diarrhea bottom and rinsing out my underwear in the toilet. I was *always* messing my pants and no matter how hard I tried, I simply could not control my bowels. This was a BIG problem for me, and as much as people would say it was something I needed to learn to control and it was just a issue of not being able to "hold it", my mother knew better. She always knew there was something just not right about all this.

Believing there was more to my problem than having

bowel issues, my mom continued to look for the answer. She persisted in having me checked for a more specific illness. At that time in the late 1950's and early 1960's pediatricians were almost non-existent.

"No, there was nothing more to this", was our family doctors' diagnosis. This is a healthy baby boy, and not to worry, he will outgrow his bowel problems, it's probably his digestive system that had not yet fully developed, and it will soon end. Much to my mother's chagrin the problem never did go away, if anything it got worse.

In addition to my bowel problems my mom was also aware that my finger nails were exceptionally large. They were certainly different from her two daughters. Plus my skin was very salty. It was an unusual taste when she kissed her child's skin or tasted my salty tears. And there was always the usual stuffed nose and I seemed to constantly be clearing my throat or coughing. Often times I would have what felt like a knot in my stomach, and it would hurt, but it seemed to always go away and I would simply forget about it until the next time I had it. I remember staying home from elementary school because of this mysterious stomach ache. These things certainly seemed unusual to my mother and father, still I had not been diagnosed with any specific illness.

Cystic fibrosis was almost unknown as a childhood illness in the 60'and 70's. There was very little written about the disease to that point. The few times my mother would find an article or small bit of information about it she would compare it to my existing problems and again talk with my doctors with no real solid answers. She narrowed my problem down to two things: celiac disease or cystic fibrosis.

Around the age of twelve I had a sweat test done on the recommendation of my new pediatrician. The test came back border line for cystic fibrosis, but nothing was confirmed and no medication was suggested or offered for my digestive problems at any time during those pre-teen or teen years.

   I'm not saying that I had some terrible childhood throughout this. My childhood was really a great time as far as I was concerned. I lived my life as normal as possible, because really I didn't know any better and I just wanted to have fun with all my cousins, classmates and friends. I knew I was different in some ways but I didn't want it to deter me from doing what any other youngster did. I just did some things more discreetly. Yes, as I got into 5th, 6th and 7th grades I became more conscious of my thin build, slow developing puberty, slight cough, large nails and smelly bowel movements, but I was sure there had to be others out there with the same problems and issues that I was experiencing.

   So these were the pieces of my puzzle that you could see or smell. Other pieces were more personal to me and my family, and really it seemed in the end, no one knew what the final picture was going to be.

An Attempt at Sports

My life went on and I became more involved in sports like many young boys. In middle school I reluctantly took a summer tennis program sponsored by our town. I fought my mom about taking the lessons, I remember absolutely, positively not wanting to go to them and being so mad I refused to talk to her on the car ride to the lessons. (I also did this with golf, I was very consistent and very stubborn). I did quite well at tennis though. At the end of the tennis program a play-off tournament was held. I certainly was not the biggest, tallest or fastest kid in the program, but I had good coordination and had learned to play tennis pretty well. This was still in the days *before* every kid got a trophy for just showing up and you actually were rewarded for doing well and not rewarded for just holding the racket. I won that whole darn tournament and when the trophies were handed out I was given the first place title. I still have that trophy today, if for no other reason than to prove I actually did it. It was during this point in my life that I realized after strenuous exercise the sweat on my arms would literally dry into a white layer of salt. I remember rubbing the salt off my arms to clear the dried whiteness away.

In high school I tried out for the football team. I was very aware of my build, although not short, I was more slight in stature. My overall body structure was just smaller than average. My wrists and arms were thin, my legs were too. I had almost no truly defined muscle definition and I couldn't seem to put on any additional weight or muscle mass even when I tried. I "played" with pants and shoulder pads that even when tied their tightest I still could easily walk out of. The coaches could not kick anyone off the football team in those days but they could decide not to play me, and that's exactly what they did. I played in few games, only those when we were ahead by enough that I could not hurt the final result of a win. I stood on the sidelines and watched much more than I played and football was not a great success for me.

I did a lot of skiing in my high school days, many nights during weekdays and all day on week-ends. I could definitely hold my own on the ski slope, but I was not able to power through those moguls like I thought I should have. When I was 17 years old, three other friends and I drove to Stowe, VT. Four seventeen year old boys driving 350 miles across New York State and into Vermont for a week of skiing. I won't even say what happened on that trip! But Stowe was unbelievable and really tested our abilities. I had no real problem there. I had good endurance and never tired of skiing the whole day long. My lungs were fine. I did not weigh much, probably only 130 lbs. at five feet ten. I just wasn't physically maturing and becoming the strong young man I thought I should be. Although I was told by my dad it would eventually happen, it did not.

Four Years at College   1975-1979

The college I attended, Rochester Institute of Technology in Rochester, New York, is an excellent engineering, photography, graphic design, printing, pottery, glass blowing and furniture design school.

My major was graphic design, so it was ideal in many ways. One, it wasn't a big school, the enrollment was approximately 12,000 undergraduate students. Two it was an excellent school for my field of study. Three it was close to home. I could make the one hour drive home every other month or so to get my laundry done, but it was still far enough away that my mom or dad would not just drop by for a unannounced visit. Although my mom thought I wouldn't be college material, apparently I was. I wasn't the most talented or smartest student but I truly enjoyed the college experience.

During my freshman year of college my doctor, Dr. Mango, suggested I have a series of tests done which I agreed to have during my college winter break. I was by this time constantly harassed at school about my oppressive smell in the bathroom and decided to take him up on the offer. I spent three glorious fun filled days in beautiful Buffalo General Hospital. I had a series of tests performed but the one I distinctly remember involved swallowing a rather large metal pill-like device attached to a thin plastic tube. I remember my mother and sister Holly were visiting me when this procedure was performed. They were asked to leave the room, which sent up a huge red flag for me, and my internal alarms started sounding. Danger, danger. I was then asked to somehow swallow this monster of a pill. This device when swallowed would make its way from my stomach into my intestines and during the natural course of digestion it would capture a bit of my intestinal fluid to be examined. I don't know if it was like the SmartPill used today that measures the acidity in a CF persons gastrointestinal tract, but I do know I spent the entire evening with this tube going down my throat with this gigantic pill attached. I could literally feel it make its way deeper and deeper into my intestines. It could feel the tug of the plastic tube on the inside of my mouth and often times down my throat on its slow journey. This was not only uncomfortable, but I believe uncomfortable to watch. I remember my father coming in to visit and staying an extremely short time and cringing each time I attempted to talk and gagged to the point of almost throwing up. That evening was 100% anxiety filled. The following morning the pill-like device was pulled back through my intestine, through my stomach, up my esophagus and out my mouth. I cannot express my relief at getting it out of my body.

"The thick mucus seen in the lungs has a counterpart in thickened secretions from the pancreas, an organ responsible for providing digestive juices that help break down food. The lack of digestive enzymes leads to difficulty absorbing nutrients with their subsequent excretion in the feces and the procedure I had was able to determine that I was not absorbing necessary nutrients but was excreting them because my pancreas was not producing the necessary digestive enzymes. This results in malabsorption which leads to malnutrition and poor growth and development because of calorie loss"[9], thus explaining my thin stature.

After the tests were analyzed a diagnosis of cystic fibrosis was determined.

This was the first time I positively knew what I had. I was now 18 years old. I have 2 copies of Delta F508 gene mutation cystic fibrosis, the most common and often fatal mutation of the disease.

Not A Life Changer

My life did not change significantly now that I knew what I actually had. I went back to college and told my roommate that I had this disease and really he was just slightly more clueless than I was about it. I knew the symptoms I had, but didn't know ANYTHING specific about the disease. Nobody told me how terrible this disease can be, so I wasn't too terribly upset knowing I had it. OK, I have these obvious bowel issues. This was the first time I was told to take any kind of medication which turned out to be enzyme pills for digestion which when properly taken would eliminate most of the bowel problems. At every meal or snack I was to take 2-3 pills to aid in digestion and reduce the foul smell of my bowel movements. Well, guess what...I didn't take them. I didn't have the discipline to take medication on a regular basis. I instead suffered for many more years thinking I did not need to take them.

Today I cannot imagine NOT taking my enzymes. They have made a huge improvement in the quality of my daily life. Today I take an enzyme drug called Creon, which breaks down the undigested fats in foods in my stomach and intestines. "The lack of digestive enzymes leads to difficulty absorbing nutrients with their subsequent excretion in the feces, which basically excretes as a wet, slimy diarrhea type bowel movement and a disorder known as malabsorption. Malabsorption leads to malnutrition and poor growth and development because of calorie loss. Individuals with CF also have difficulties absorbing the fat-soluble vitamins A, D, E, and K. A multi-vitamin formulated specially for CF'ers is taken to get these vitamins into their bodies."[9] At that time however I didn't want to be bothered. I was essentially a young, fairly healthy male with stinky bowel movements.

I was also a young stupid male because…..

often times I smoked. Although I was never a full time smoker I did it based on the fact that all my roommates smoked. Wasn't that reason enough?

Smoking is dangerous, in and of itself. It can kill you, but with cystic fibrosis it truly is a deadly combination. Did I mention how stupid I was in college?

A Meeting to Remember

My best friend Brad went to college in Utica, New York. The college, Mohawk Valley Community College was a perfect place for him. It was a great two year "starter" college where you could get your feet wet in a college environment, but it wasn't so competitive that you felt the stress often associated with a big school college atmosphere. I know he made a lot of good, lasting friendships at this school. And because it was in Utica, he was away from home in a college setting and not in his backyard of parental control at our local community college. I remember visiting him only once. He lived in the upstairs of a very old, beat-up house. I remember the floors slanted to one direction. The house was cold, drafty and not at all like the townhouse that was presently my residence in Rochester. I'm sure if you lived for a period of time in the house, you could make it a home. As much as I was glad to visit him, I was more than glad to leave, not him of course, but the house.

He often mentioned a friend he had met there who was from the Buffalo area. His name was Rick and I believe he was one of Brad's floor mates for a period of time. He told me Rick had cystic fibrosis also and Brad knew he had it before Rick ever told him. Rick had fingernails that were clubbed, like most cystics. Brad always called my fingernails "moonmen". (More on that later). Anyway, Rick was surprised Brad even knew what cystic fibrosis was and even more surprised that Brad knew another person with it. Brad would come home during a college break and tell me how much sicker Rick was than me, and how he couldn't believe we had the same disease. He told me of his last Spring Break when he and some of his friends, including Rick drove to Florida. Rick apparently tried to hide his illness from the others, but it was hard. He was one sick young man and it's hard to hide a constant, thick wet cough and a portable oxygen tank.

Brad and Rick stayed friends during college and he would tell me of his constant trips into the hospital for his "tune ups". One day when I was home from school the doorbell rang and there was Brad and Rick. I was standing face to face with another person with cystic fibrosis. It was the first time I ever met another person with this disease. We didn't know what to say, or how to act and I treated the meeting as if nothing was out of the ordinary or unusual. Rick was very thin like most cystics and he had the barrel chest, another common cystic trait, but otherwise he seemed like any man in his early 20's.

I never saw Rick after that day, but I never forgot him. Rick had a double lung/heart transplant less than a year after I met him. He was one of the first people to ever have such a radical surgery. I remember reading the news article of his transplant in the paper. There was a picture of him, smiling. I still have the news clipping somewhere. Rick died a very short time after his transplant. I believe he lived just a few days.

Rick was the first person I knew with cystic fibrosis and the first person I knew to die of cystic fibrosis. It really made me realize the gravity of the disease I had and how lucky I had been up to that point.

Is There Life After College? 1979-1981

Anyway, my life barreled on, I graduated from the RIT in May, 1979 with a degree in Fine and Applied Arts, which essentially meant I could work in an advertising agency or design studio as a graphic designer, art director or, and this is what happened in my case, a paste-up artist. A paste up artist is the person who prepares the ad or brochure or business card or whatever for print production. They do NOT design the ad, brochure or business card. Design is what I went to college to do, not paste-up!

There is a fine line between understanding what is necessary for the job world and not understanding what is necessary. My roommate during college seemed to understand, I did not. He was more prepared for the cruel world, I was not. What was the difference between us? Well, very little, but there was a difference. He learned how to use his talent wisely, how to cut corners when it was beneficial, how to make things work in his favor and not try to force something to work for him, how to ADAPT to the situation. He was using less effort yet getting better results. I was more rigid, working harder and getting poorer results. Let me tell you, college only prepares you for the real world in the most abstract sense. Never once did any of my professors teach us how to work smart, I could have used that advice. I finally learned it, but I learned it the hard way. I eventually learned it on the job.

Unfortunately at that time, internships were not a common component of my college curriculum. Our program in Fine and Applied Arts did not have an internship program, so I believed I missed out on a great opportunity to learn and experience in the work day environment. Today an internship is very common and in some cases necessary in order to receive a degree in your field of study.

After graduation I ended up living once again at home, feeling very frustrated and confined. I had essentially lived on my own the last four years, not counting coming home for good meals, getting my laundry done and summer vacations of course. I was not prepared for the blandness and conformity of home life. What happened to the keg parties, the guys coming over at virtually any hour for fun and more fun. The girls, where were the girls! I loved my mom, but really, I wanted to go back to school! I believe to this day this is one of the reasons people stay in school. The real working world is no picnic, school however can be a great never-ending social picnic.

Still my disease seemingly posed no negative effects on me. Apart from the stinky bowel movements and the often excruciating pain from my sometimes clogged intestinal tract I was OK.

I was now running with my sisters; almost every day I would go for a jog, two, three miles a day. Running is one of those things that once you get over the hump of the soreness and learning the breathing and where and when to exert yourself, it is actually pretty addicting. My leg muscles got strongest during my running days, but still my definition was never great and my calves never were very pronounced like many of the other runners I would see. I ran in many 5K races (3.1 miles), but I was never competitive, not even a little.

My job search at home now was going nowhere. I interviewed for many positions of graphic designer but was not able to break that barrier into the advertising world. I was still keeping up with many of the guys I hung with in college although it seemed they were the ones that were working. My college roommate had a graphic design job in Palo Alto, California, a superb designers dream location. At that time, in the early 80's Palo Alto was home to some of the best graphic design studios in the country. Another college buddy was in New York City, and he was working for a small design studio, doing exactly what we had be taught in college, another was in Boca Raton, FL, whose soon to be wife was working for IBM.

I was frustrated, anxious and ready to make a move. After talking one day with my friend Eli, who was working in New York City he convinced me, which didn't take too much, to bust out of Buffalo and head to the Big Apple. It was now the early 80's. I moved into Eli's one bedroom apartment on East 86th St. A great building, a great apartment, a great neighborhood. I slept on his couch, and we got along well for quite a while. The bad thing about two guys occupying a one bedroom apartment is you have nowhere to hide. There's nowhere to go and be by yourself and in many respects that was true for my accommodating roommate. Although he had his own bedroom, every time he left it to go to the kitchen or living room, there I was. Eventually it got tough on us both.

Finally I got a job as that paste-up artist. I was making just enough to move out and that's what I did. I moved from NYC to Long Island. I went from taking a 10 minute subway ride to taking an hour and ten minute Long Island Railroad commute. But I had my own place on the third floor of a home in Elmont, NY, just about five minutes from the Belmont racetrack. I had to get up with the sun to catch the train into Manhattan, but like everyone else I got used to it and honestly it was a great time to catch up on a well needed snooze on the ride into the city.

So I guess my life was slowly moving ahead, I was barely surviving financially, had few friends on Long Island, and had little knowledge of, or effect from my cystic fibrosis.

A Trip to Sanibel   March, 1982

I think I had been working just over a year in Manhattan when my family decided to take a vacation to Sanibel Island, FL. I flew from LaGuardia Airport and my mom and sister, Holly flew from Buffalo and we met in Ft. Myers, FL. It was great to get away and relax. At that time my work vacation was limited to just one week.

One afternoon my sister who had gotten her masters in Pediatric Pulmonary Care nursing and I were playing around on the floor of the condo we had rented. I was lying flat and she wanted to look up my nose. I had been complaining of a pinkish sac like obstruction in my nasal cavity that I could not only feel but see when I looked in a mirror and up my nose. Honestly, it was not only weird to see but disgusting.

Yep, she was sure, as she examined me, it was nasal polyps. Nasal polyps are common for a person with CF. "Nasal polyps affect between 10-50% of people with CF. Polyps are small, sac-like growths of inflamed nasal mucosa (masses in the nose) that are caused by chronic inflammation in the nasal lining. Examined under a microscope, nasal polyps are essentially bags of tissue and fluid. The exact cause of nasal polyps is unknown but allergy, infections and chronic congestion often play a key role. Most people with nasal polyps complain of nasal blockage which affects both sides of the nose (not to the same extent). Other symptoms include runny nose, loss of sense of smell, facial pain or congestion and nose bleeds (less common)."[4]

Eventually I had a simple surgical procedure – a polypectomy. "A polypectomy removes the polyps to relieve nasal obstruction. There are rare surgical risks including bleeding and impact to the eyes and brain. Major benefits are an enhanced sense of smell, decreased nasal/facial pain and congestion."[4]

I had the procedure done at Children's Hospital of Buffalo (now called Women and Children's Hospital of Buffalo). Not only did I have the polyps removed I had my sinuses scraped. At that point I basically lost my ability to smell, and cannot smell today. My polyps however, have never returned. I still have nasal congestion but I do not have any serious nasal bacterial infections which make CF lungs susceptible to infection or colonization.

NYC - San Fran. – Buffalo - NYC 1982-1985

I eventually left New York and headed to San Francisco to join my college roommate who was working in Palo Alto. I got the "this place is great" song and dance and bit. He lived just outside Oakland in a nice community called Piedmont. My new roommate (actually old, from college), Mark also had a one bedroom apartment, and again I slept on his couch. Since I had lived with Mark in college he was easier to get along with and although we didn't agree on everything we coped with the close quarters well.

Eventually I got a full time job in San Francisco at the San Francisco Clean Water Department as a graphic artist. Mark and I moved to south Alameda County to a community called Newark, California.

We rented a house, it was a small three bedroom ranch style home with a attached garage and fenced in backyard. Our living room window looked out onto a horse farm, and we could see the horses grazing in the pasture with the rolling hills in the background. It was nice. I took BART (Bay Area Rapid Transit) into the city each day which took around one hour.

I would always go out for lunch when I worked in the City of San Francisco, and to one place in particular. It was a sandwich shop directly adjacent to City Hall. I could easily walk there from my office building. The people working there eventually got to know my face and that is where I contracted hepatitis. This was a time when preparers of food simply did not wear sanitary gloves to guard against contamination. I called my mom one day from a pay phone (they had pay phones way back then) and told her something was definitely wrong with me. Her advice was to go to a hospital ER which I did. The doctor examined me, asked a few questions and then asked if I was gay. It was after all, San Francisco. I wasn't gay but I did have hepatitis. Apparently gay men contract this disease with sexual intercourse. I had Hepatitis A, which I contracted from fecal matter; that's the gay connection.

When you get hepatitis, man you know you're sick. There wasn't, and I still don't think there is today, anything medically you can do for hepatitis except to let it run its' course. Its' course unfortunately is slow, it took me about a year to recover from that disease. I remember all I could eat was sponge cake! It was the only thing that would not make me nauseous. The disease took a huge toll on my body, I lost a lot of weight and eventually I moved back home to Buffalo and back with my mom (thank g-d for my mom) who made sponge cake until it was coming out of her ears.

I couldn't seem to get my career moving in the Buffalo area although I did have a few in my profession of graphic design that didn't amount to anything.

One day I just called my old employer in Manhattan. My old boss said I was always welcome back so that's where I headed; back to New York City. I was now 25 years old. I moved back to Long Island to a town called Freeport, New York on the south shore of the Long Island. I could actually ride my bike to the Atlantic Ocean and often times I did.

The apartment I lived in was right on the edge of the seedier part of town. And the complex I moved into was a zoo of humanity. I immediately knew this was probably going to be an adventure to remember. And it was.

I the first night I slept in my apartment someone shot a bullet through my bedroom window. I moved my bed the next day against the corner wall where nothing coming through my windows could hit me. The woman who lived there prior to me left the place a dirty, disgusting mess. She also left herself in the apartment as apparently she had died in it and was eventually found by the landlord.

An older husband and wife lived above me. The woman

was seriously schizophrenic. When she and her husband were finally kicked out of the apartment complex I went up to see what the place looked like empty and there was a ton of garbage in it. Narrow paths to each room were formed by a wall of trash maybe 5 feet high. You could not get into her kitchen at all and, no lie because I saw it, her dog had died in the corner! They never knew it until the garbage was cleaned out. It took two large 20 foot long dumpsters to clean out just one small apartment. The whole time those people lived above me I had a cockroach problem that was unending. Those cockroaches literally threw parties in my kitchen. I would sit on my coach and watch them walk across my living room floor like they owned the place. Unreal.

One morning around 6 am I was woken by someone pounding on my door, then mysteriously they were gone.

One day a guy came to my door with a baseball bat telling me someone was trying to break into my car but he had scared them away. I was actually nervous to do my laundry at night because I had to go to another building's basement to have it done. It was crazy there.

At some point I made up my mind that New York City, San Francisco or anywhere else was not going to be my permanent home. I eventually moved back to Buffalo to look for a serious long term job and career. It took another two years before I got that career job at Benderson Development Company, Inc. a family owned commercial and industrial real estate developer, with corporate headquarters in Buffalo, NY. I was still in good health, except for the hepatitis episode, little did I know the worst was yet to come.

Cystic Fibrosis and Bowel Problems

"Much to the chagrin and embarrassment of CF patients everywhere, bowel movements are an important part of our lives. In many ways our bowel movements serve as a benchmark that lets us know how things are going, so to speak, with our digestive systems. Cystic fibrosis patients with pancreatic insufficiency are especially aware of all things related to their digestive process, and should be able to identify what's normal for them and what isn't. When the pancreas is too blocked by mucus, it can't deliver the enzymes necessary to break down the foods we eat, particularly proteins and fats. As a result, people with CF may have more frequent bowel movements because they are not absorbing the protein and fat that they are eating. As if that weren't embarrassing enough, CF patients are also prone to flatulence (gas). Their gas and BMs can be particularly foul-smelling as the result of proteins and fats not being absorbed by the body."[5]

I was always having a bowel movement. They were soft and runny and greasy and worst of all, SMELLY. Before my diagnosis my mom tried different foods hoping that she would discover the diet that best suited my problem, but it seemed as though nothing worked. She took me to doctors but there was nothing that they knew of to give me to make the problem go away. In the dark ages of time, that would be the 60's, 70's and 80's for many of you, there was no internet. The only reference material available to my mom was the library or the occasional magazine or newspaper article and the doctors expertise. And really, if a doctor didn't ever see a kid with CF, they often didn't know what the hell I had going on. I don't know if there was even any reference books on CF at that time, it was a disease most people just didn't know or know enough about.

Believe me, my youth was not easy in many ways.

Mornings were spent on the toilet, greasy bowel movements were the norm. By the time I got to school I had to go again. And I knew they stunk, in my mind I can still smell them. I would sit in the coat closet in kindergarten, literally afraid to move, for fear of messing my pants, for fear of being embarrassed. It was a rare day that I did not mess my pants, and I probably messed them almost every day. Imagine messing your pants every day for the first 3 years of school from age five through eight. To this day, I am 54 now, I can still remember the feeling. I had smelly bowel movements up until I started taking digestive enzymes to help my body absorb the fats from ingested foods. With the enzymes I was able to control my frequency, smell, amount and absorption of food. The absorption of food also helped me control my body weight and body fat more, typically people with CF are thin as they cannot absorb fat into their bodies and cannot retain much body fat.

When I was in 3rd grade, I got a pair of work boots. They were tan leather ones that laced up to the ankle. I was so proud of them. My mom let me wear them to school one day and I was really excited. It was however, not a good day otherwise. I messed my pants that day and it smelled. I remember the kids around me telling the teacher about this terrible odor and the teacher stopped the class and walked all around the room, then around my desk smelling for the cause of the problem. I just sat there with the heel of my new work boot jammed into my butt as I sat on it hoping to g-d I would not be called out as the problem of the smell. I think the teacher eventually thought it was dog poop on some ones shoe and miraculously I escaped onto the bus for that unpleasant ride home with the mess in my pants. My sister Holly, would walk down to my bus-stop, which in those days really was a long walk. There was no such thing as the school bus limousine service they have today. Being picked up at your front door is no big deal today and is what parents and children expect. Anyway, I would get on her back and she would literally carry me home (thank-you Holly). The embarrassment of those days still continues to live deep in my thoughts of my youth.

Even at ages 12, 13 and 14 I was having problems holding my bowels. Who has problems like that at such an old age? I'll tell you who…ME! Ugh.

In college, although I had finally been diagnosed with CF, I was too stupid and too undisciplined to take my enzymes. I would never go to the bathroom on my own dorm floor. I learned early on that you got teased terribly if you stunk up the bathroom. I would go to another floor, another building if I had to. If I went to another floor and there was someone using that bathroom I would keep looking until I found one empty.

The best place to go was at the college cafeteria bathroom after hours. The cafeteria building was separated from every other building. The bathrooms were located in the common area outside the cafeteria. The student cafeteria was only occupied for the breakfast, lunch and dinner college diners. I was always surprised that they didn't lock the doors after hours but the common area was always open and I used it often.

One evening I went to the dorm building next to ours and went into the bathroom on the ground floor. This was another good place as the bathroom was off the elevator lobby and most people did not know it was there. While I was using it someone walked in and occupied the stall next to me. After a minute or so, he said to me " Man buddy, you're shit really stinks!" He was right, it did stink.

You never are so acutely aware of where a bathroom is located in a home or building until you have bowel problems. Bowel issues stink!

Because with almost every bowel movement I had diarrhea, it came out with a loud noise, followed by a horrific smell. (I'm sorry if you find this explanation gross and disgusting; it was, yet it was a very large facet of my daily life and if I didn't explain what it was like I wouldn't be explaining my life with CF).

If the bathroom you were using was in close proximity to people (it always was) it was impossible to go comfortably. I became so uncomfortable going to the bathroom in someone else's home or a public place that even when there was no one around it was difficult to go. It was a hell I will never forget. To this day, it is still an issue, but today with my enzymes (three with every meal, at least one or two with a snack) that I take every time I consume food, it is controllable. My bowel movements still have a worse than average odor to them, but now they are whole and formed, and I only have one bowel movement a day instead of five, six or seven.

When I was young and had a bowel movement I would feel something protrude out of my anus. I remember using the bathroom one time, feeling the protrusion and looking under my legs and sure enough, there it was! It would then go back in after I was done. I would tell my mother and she could not really understand it or perhaps did not fully believe it was happening. Years later, when I was a young adult I was reading about CF in a book and came across a section about this effect. It is called rectal prolapse and is basically when the inside of your anus "falls out" during a bowel movement. It is most common in CF'ers under the age of 6 years old and may cause slight bleeding. I never got the bleeding, but I did experience the rectal prolapse. I had rectal prolapse until around 12 years old. Although I no longer have it, it is something I will never forget.

Cystic Fibrosis and Clubbed Finger

I always have had big nails. "This condition's precise cause is uncertain, although it has been observed in people with other serious lung diseases such as emphysema, lung cancer or bronchiectasis. Some in the medical community suspect that the formation of excess tissue, similar to that occurring with bronchiectasis, has something to do with the body's imbalance of the specific protein that stimulates

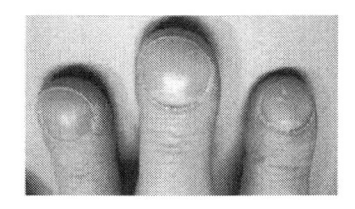

My friend Brad always said my fingernails looked like "moonmen".
Notice the similarity.

muscle growth. This seems to make sense, especially for cystic fibrosis patients who are usually deficient in calcium - a nutrient required not only for bone strength, but for the proper formation and function of muscle tissue."[16]

My best friend Brad called my fingers "moon men". Instead of my fingers tapering at the end, they are wider at the end, looking a bit like clubs. In reality my fingers are not as pronounced as other people with CF. Some have excessive sized nails and they really don't look like their fingers fit their hands. Almost all cystics have this condition of clubbed fingers. The moon men thing began because my nails look a bit like the face shield of Buzz Aldrin's helmet as he walked on the surface of the moon. If you can remember back that far (I can), it is a big face shield and he's standing facing the camera. It became a famous photo of him, hence the "moon men" metaphor. Over the years I've had numerous people tell me how big my nails were. It's as though they are telling me something I didn't know. Believe me I KNOW! My toes are even worse. The big toe is quite large, and I won't ever take my shoes and socks off in front of someone who doesn't know me well. My family is accustomed to my nails; others stare as though they have just seen someone with monsters feet. I remember going swimming once at my friends' house. There was a woman I invited to go swimming. She was someone I worked with, and I remember her looking at my feet with utter amazement as though she was seeing someone from a freak show in a circus. I know I was the talk of the office the next day to her work friends. Oh well, I guess we're not perfect, not one of us.

Cystic Fibrosis and Coughing

"Cystic fibrosis (CF) is a multisystem disease which impacts the digestive system, sweat glands, and the reproductive tract, but progressive pulmonary insufficiency continues to be major cause of morbidity and mortality. The main respiratory manifestations include chronic bacterial colonization, cough, bronchiectasis, haemoptysis, emphysema, and pneumothorax. As the disease progresses chronic cough becomes a universal symptom, reported by virtually all patients."[3]

It wasn't unusual for me to feel very anxious at social events, including parties, my daughter's school or extra-curricular events, movies or religious events to name just a few. I was very self-conscious because I was always coughing. You know people are aware of it. You know they don't say anything, but are probably wondering if I have a cold and they will catch one or question that I'm a smoker and I have a smokers cough. I can't say I blamed them. Not knowing my situation, I might have felt the same.

My cough was always a constant intrusion into my life, it was always there. I would try to get as much of the junk out of my lungs as possible before I entered into a social situation so I didn't cough immediately. Of course, it would not be long before I did cough, and then it was a matter of how much sputum actually was cleared out of my lungs. It was always a thick, wet disgusting cough. If I did not clear it out with the first or second cough, I was in trouble because there was more where that came from. It would build up in my lungs and the next cough would be even thicker and wetter and more disgusting. There were times I just could not clear my lungs and it would build up to the point when finally I did cough it up and it was thick and sticky and a lot. I would have to swallow it, a big clump of it and everyone around me must have thought I was the heaviest smoker or had the worst cold.

At the movies I would save up my biggest, hardest cough for the part when the audience was laughing or the point when the movie was the loudest, there was almost always some of those, or at one of my daughter's recitals or choral concerts when everyone was clapping. Those moments hid a lot of uncomfortable coughing situations. It was a brutal issue for me and happened at every social event I can remember. It was truly one of the most scary personal issues I had to deal with.

It's funny when you realize which circumstances in your life effect you so greatly while other people don't even give the same circumstance a second thought. I have learned to not judge people by these factors as you really don't know the situation behind it and cannot make an accurate judgment based on what you see or hear.

I remember when I was in junior high school (middle school) and my teacher moved me from the front of the class to the back because she said I gave her a cold from my constant coughing. I told my mother about this and she was very upset. I was not diagnosed with CF at this point in time, but she was aware that my coughing was not cold related. I know she felt this was an unfair assessment of me and yes it was, based on what this teacher perceived to be, but not on what was actually true.

My wife used to tell me she could find me in a grocery or department store by my cough. It was like leaving bread crumbs on the path to find your way home, my cough was her way of finding me in a store full of aisles of merchandise. This is how much a person with CF coughs. They will do it every few seconds or perhaps every couple of minutes and it is a distinctive sound. Easy to recognize, easy to find.

I often look at old photos of me, many with my daughter Mikaela and my wife, many of the photos when Mikaela is very young and I think to myself, "that was taken with

42

my old lungs, or "that was when I had my OWN lungs".

I look at those pictures and remember what I felt at that exact moment when the picture was taken. I cannot believe how normal I looked in these pictures but recalling how absolutely lousy I felt.

When I got home soon after my transplant my wife would comment on how quiet the house was even though I was in it. They was no longer the sound of my persistent cough. That was a real eye opener to me on what an impact my disease had and still does make on our daily family life.

She's no Biotch   November 1994

   I had been working at Benderson Development Co., a privately owned commercial and industrial real estate developer for probably 11 years when the in-house advertising agency in which I was the head graphic designer, (yeah me, finally the head designer)! hired a new account executive. Word around the agency was that she was a bitch and her name was Deborah. I was never into forming opinions about people until I had at least a few personal experiences with them. I first met her in my office when I was introduced to her by my boss. She seemed fine. I must admit, I especially liked her blue eyes and she had beautiful skin. I thought she was probably Italian.
   It didn't take long before my decision about Deborah was made up. She was no bitch. She was a nice, sincere and talented account executive. Honestly, I wanted to get to know Deborah more. I eventually learned that she was actually of Italian and Syrian background and her faith was Jewish.
   I gave Deborah a lot of extra attention, I often paid for her lunches as she seemed to travel with no cash on her what-so-ever. I drove her to and from work (we happened to live in the same neighborhood). I even followed her home from work once during a snowstorm as she was afraid she could get stuck. This was before cell phones. Eventually we dated here and there and as charming as I was, she would not commit to seeing just me. It drove me nuts!
   Deborah led me on my chase, and so it went. I think I finally broke her down after almost two years of free lunches. Finally she accepted my marriage proposal and another free lunch of barbecued chicken fingers.

Married with Diabetes   August 1997

Deborah and I got married in August of 1997. At our wedding I saw some friends that I had not seen in quite a while. Guys I grew up with that were now living out of town and were nice enough to come back for our wedding. I will never forget one particular friend saying to me "So, what's going on with you? You've always been thin, but I don't remember you ever being this thin". I shrugged it off that night, but honestly I had noticed that not only was I thinner, I could not put on any muscle weight from working out and just working out was, well work.

We went on our honeymoon to Aruba. I don't believe I ever bothered to really look at myself in a mirror or thought to weigh myself before. So it never occurred to me that perhaps something was seriously going on with my body that needed looking into. I distinctly remember snorkeling at this secluded spot in Aruba one day and looking down at my body and particularly my stomach. I had NO fat. No love handles, no spare tire, no anything. It wasn't all muscle either. I felt and looked literally like skin and bones at least with just a bathing suit on. I decided that the discussion of how thin I was had to be brought up on my next clinic visit. At my next appointment, which at that time were still six months apart, my doctors and I discussed the situation and with a little blood work the answer to my problem was solved. I had cystic fibrosis-related diabetes.

"Diabetes is a very common complication that develops over time in many people with cystic fibrosis. In fact, most adults living with CF have some degree of diabetes or glucose intolerance. Cystic fibrosis — related diabetes (CFRD) is a unique type of diabetes that only people with cystic fibrosis can get. CFRD is similar to, but not the same as, diabetes in people who do not have cystic fibrosis.

Diabetes in people with cystic fibrosis combines the characteristics of both type 1 and type 2 diabetes. Build up of thick secretions in the pancreas eventually damages the hormone-producing cells, causing insulin deficiency. This sounds like type 1 diabetes, but it is not quite the same thing because it does not start in childhood, but in adulthood, and is caused by damage to a pancreas that used to produce insulin normally. In addition to insulin deficiency, people with cystic fibrosis often wind up with insulin resistance because of chronic infections, high levels of cortisol, a hormone that the body secretes in response to stress and frequent exposure to corticosteroids, which are anti-inflammatory drugs sometimes used in the treatment of lung conditions."[2]

I was put on an insulin pill for a time, I think it was about a year in which time it had little positive results. I then was put on insulin injection therapy which I must admit was a bit scary at first. A visiting nurse came to my home to go over the teaching process of checking my insulin blood levels and injecting myself with the insulin pen and tracking my insulin numbers. She was explaining where I could most comfortably inject myself and when she saw the amount of belly fat I had her response was, "Well, you don't really have much (fatty tissue) to inject there, so you'll have to inject yourself in the leg, thigh or lower back (butt) area". I was basically skin and bones!

After getting used to this new routine I started to gain some weight and got out of the real danger zone of being too underweight for the seriousness of my illness. Many years later, my CF doctor made it a priority for his patients to really work on keeping as much body weight on as possible. Research showed that this helped in the overall health, especially lung health of a cystic fibrosis individual.

Today I inject myself with insulin almost every time I eat or drink something. That is often 4-5 times a day. It can really be a pain in the butt (where I also inject myself), but at this time I don't want an insulin pump and would prefer to use a pen syringe instead. I also give myself Lantus insulin which is a long acting insulin. This keeps my insulin levels are a more even keel during a 24 hour period.

  It took a long time for me to find Deborah and I am thankful we are together as husband and wife. Now I have to work even harder to stay healthy. CF with diabetes is going to be a struggle, but with Deb by my side it will be a struggle I do not have to fight alone.

My First "Tune Up" January, 2000

The first time I went into the hospital for a "tune up" was in January of 2000. For those who are not familiar with the terminology, a "tune up" is a term used in the cystic fibrosis community to refer to a preventive course of intravenous antibiotics and respiratory therapy. Depending on the doctor's preference and the specific case of the individual with CF, a "tune up" can last from 2 to 4 weeks. "Usually a tune up is started in the hospital, where the CF specialist and team can keep a close eye on things with regard to dosages of antibiotics, and any changes in pulmonary function."[18] My wife was 4 months pregnant with our first child. I remember going to the CF doctor for my regular three month visit and at the past few appointments he was politely warning me to expect a hospital stay in the very near future. Apparently my PFT's were trending downward and he felt it was better to head off the disease before it got ahead of me. So during my December appointment my physician said the words that I really thought I would not hear at that time,
 "I recommend you go into the hospital for a "tune up". I was shaken by the request to go into the hospital, scared by the fact I was actually sick enough to have to go in and it completely caught me off guard. It took some time to process the request. I went back to work, talked with my sister on the phone about it and discussed it with my wife Deborah later when I got home. She was also surprised by it too, I remember her saying to me tearfully, "I thought this time wouldn't be here yet, you weren't that sick yet, I thought you told me you wouldn't be going into the hospital yet". But I was wrong, I was going in. The weird thing was I believed I was OK, nothing was wrong and my doctor was over-reacting.

The days prior to going in, I would call or talk with my sisters and mother on the phone and literally be crying. I believed this was all a mistake, like arresting someone for a crime they didn't commit. But the doctors at Women and Children's Hospital were telling it like it was time and eventually I came to the realization that I did need to go in. At 41 years old my life was changing dramatically.

The first day in, I got the only room available on the 10th floor with its' own bathroom and its own shower. All the other rooms had common shared showers accessed off the hallways.

My first hour there was a flurry of nurses and a physician's assistant who guided me through what the hospital stay would entail. Hospital employees would come in, introduce themselves and say, "Oh, you're new, I don't remember you ever visiting us." I never had. An adult first timer was unusual and for a while I felt like the bearded lady in the circus. I was the rarity that everyone wanted to see.

I was told I had a choice of a PICC (peripherally inserted central catheter) line or an intravenous (IV) line which was how my medications would be delivered, a PICC line would last indefinitely, an intravenous line would last 3-4 days. What a PICC line was, I didn't have a clue. A PICC line for those who also don't know is a tiny, tiny tube they snake into a peripheral vein, usually in the arm at about the inside elbow. An insertion point that is higher up on the arm is better as the veins are larger and insertion somewhat easier. First the insertion point is numbed, either by a jell of lidocream or by an injection of lidocaine that stings like a bee sting. The whole area is sterilized and an incision is made into the skin and then into the vein. The line is inserted into your vein and travels up your arm and makes a U-turn into your chest where it happily stays and delivers your medication directly into your bloodstream for the best and quickest impact. They measure the line length prior to insertion and X-ray you for proper placement once it's inserted.

The total length of a PICC line for me was about 20 inches, maybe a bit less. For a child it may be about a foot. When the treatment is complete they pull it out. A doctor or nurse can pull it out, I prefer a certified PICC nurse specialist.

I wanted to go with the plain intravenous line, but was told this was not the best option and after much deliberation went with the PICC. I can't put into words how unhappy I was about this whole thing. Since that first PICC, I have had probably eight more inserted at various visits to the hospital.

I remember them taking my blood oxygen level from my finger and it read 99%. The nurse said it couldn't be better and I felt even more confused as to why I was in this predicament. I spent a week in the hospital receiving antibiotics and being introduced to chest PT by hand and by the vest. My wife stayed with me the first night and I think another night sometime during that week. It was tough on her, but she is a person that rarely complains or over-worries and I could always count on her during these difficult times.

My in-laws still did not know about my disease and they did not know about this hospital visit. Only my physician, my immediate family and my wife knew of my CF. I was able to go home for one evening and watch the Super Bowl with Deborah, the Saint Louis Rams against the Tennessee Titans, but I had to leave at halftime and went back to the hospital and watched the rest of the game in my room on that crappy television hanging from the wall. The Rams won 23-16. After 7 days I was discharged.

Between 1997 and 2001, there were two adult CF doctors on staff at Children's Hospital. One of the doctors had been there for a few years and was slightly less proactive in his CF treatment methods and another; Dr. Cronin that was new to the lung center staff. Dr. Cronin was very proactive in his treatment methods. He was the doctor who recommended I go into the hospital for my "tune up". Both doctors were young men, very bright and knowledgeable in treating the disease, but they had somewhat different methodologies of approaching the illness. I wasn't aware of it at the time but the doctor who had been treating the adult CF'ers for many years was the one who discharged me. Dr. Cronin apparently would not have approved of my discharge, and I remember him being quite upset when he found out that I had been given my walking papers.

I ended up going home with the PICC line still in my arm and doing self-medicated anti-biotics at home. This was the only time during my many years going into WCHOB that I went home with a PIC in my arm and I gave myself IV antibiotics for another week. When the week was up a visiting nurse came into my home and removed the line. All the rest of my hospital visits were two weeks or more and my PIC was taken out in the hospital when my stay was complete. After that first "tune up" I was good for another year and a half before I went into the hospital again.

My Perfect Gift   May 24, 2000

It's a beautiful, crisp day today. The sun is out but a jacket is necessary as the breeze has a slight chill to it. Today is a very special and exciting day for both Deb and I. Deborah is having a planned C-section today and we are having our first child. We decided not to learn the sex of our baby, we do not have a preference of a boy or a girl. (I have a preference, I want a girl). Deb and I picked the 24th of May because we were married on the 24th of August.

It is not always easy to have a baby when you have cystic fibrosis. The cystic body was not built to have kids, not that it's impossible, it's just more complicated for most. But thanks to some incredible doctors and a bit of luck, on May 24th at 12:24 pm we were blessed with a baby girl. We named her Mikaela Fay. As thrilled as I was to be a new father, always in the back of my mind was the thought of my illness and how it will impact the lives of my new baby girl and my wife. I am tremendously happy yet very concerned.

We brought our new baby daughter home on May 27th and I began my official role as father. I was 43 years old. Old for a new father definitely, old for a cystic, most definitely.

Deep Blue to Bright Red

My interpretation of the life of a Cystic Fibrosis individual. What we strive to be and what we want other people to see us as, not just what's on the outside but what's on the inside as well:

THE RAINBOW HORSE

Long ago, or so it seems,
in a far-away place called the land of your dreams,
lived a horse of many colors, in a meadow with trees,
great mountains above, a warm scented sea breeze.

This horse was different from the rest of her friends,
they were brown, black and white with one a grey blend.
Her coat was rainbow, deep blue to bright red,
which made her quite different and so it is said.

Long ago in this land far away,
Rainbow Horse loved to laugh, dance and play.
Deep blue to bright red and all colors between,
Rainbow Horses' happiness was not what it seemed.

She felt different from many, not common at all,
she shone like a sunbeam in a deep winter's squall.
Sometimes another would laugh and make fun,
"Rainbow Horse isn't like us, no, not one".

"Oh how I wish I was just like the rest,
being one color is what I request".
"To be plain and simple, to be really quite bland,
like the white in the clouds, the color of sand".

Now there lived a wise Oak in this land far away,
a bright beacon to follow and not turn astray.

The wise Oak asked Rainbow Horse a question so true,
"Do you want to know why, do you wonder why you?"

"You're unique in a 'Rainbow Horse' kind of way,
with a coat that's different from the usual grey".
"Your uniqueness makes you, and each one of them too,
for each horse is like no other, and no others like you".

"Each horse makes this meadow a really fun place,
you'll never see double when you look in a face".
"One has long ears, another's tail is curly,
one likes to stay up late, one gets up too early.
One loves to eat candy, one enjoys only toast,
one is little and smaller than most.
One is quite lazy and likes staying in bed,
one is rainbow colors, deep blue to bright red".

Now the wise Oak was right, but had more to explain,
Rainbow Horse listened closely, there was still more to gain.
"Deep blue to bright red are the colors you see,
but the colors inside you are the colors to be".

"Kind and honest, fair and true,
these are the colors that make up the real you".
"Treat everyone you meet in just the same way,
and happiness will fill you as light fills the day".

"Now be happy you're different, one of a kind,
there's only one you, a treasure, a find".

The wise Oak was done, he'd completed his task,
Rainbow Horse was ready to remove her sad mask.
She was proud of her coat, unlike any other,
but the beauty inside her was the gift to discover.

When she was told she was different, not like the rest,
she did not hang her head, she was up to the test.
She smiled and said "thank-you, that is really quite nice"
"You noticed my difference, you had to look twice".

But what makes me so special, if that's what you seek,
is the color inside me that makes me unique.
Kind and honest, fair and true,
these are my true colors, not the red and the blue.

Long ago, or so it seems,
in a far-away place called the land of your dreams,
lived a horse of many colors who loved to laugh, dance and play,
and now happiness fills her as light fills the day.

I wrote this poem for my daughter Mikaela when she was around 5 years old. I wrote this story using a girl horse so my daughter could connect with it a bit better.

This poem is my interpretation of my unique life with Cystic Fibrosis in a world that doesn't really understand it. You know having cystic fibrosis is a battle but we must try to handle our disease as our uniqueness and not our downfall.

I...I...I...I'm Stayin' Alive, Stayin' Alive
(Sung to the Bee Gee's Song Only)
April, 2001

I'm back in the hospital for a "tune up". Although I'm not in bad shape, my doctor wants to keep me as healthy as possible for as long as possible. I believe I'm doing pretty well. I made it just over a year without going back into the hospital. I'm sure this visit will be a two week stay, my first two weeker ever. The room I stayed in during my first visit has been converted to a sleep apnea study room, so it's no longer available.

I'm in the new suite now. When I first got here I was in a typical single room as another CF'er was in the new suite. That patient has now left the suite, I assume they've gone home. Since I was here last they have completed and opened this suite room for CF patients only. Basically they took two single rooms and made it into one big suite type room. It's nice, it has a couch that folds out into a bed, a nice comfy chair, a couple end tables, a dining table, the TV swivels on the wall so you can watch it from any part of the room. The private bathroom is big with a shower. The paint is new, the floor is new and clean and the view is a great one of downtown Buffalo. It's designed for the long haul. Not bad for a bad situation.

The Hospital Routine   December, 2003

This is the fourth time I've be in for a "tune up". My FEV1 is 37% and my FVC is 77%. I have gotten used to the routine here now. Usually I have had an appointment in the lung clinic, have my PFT's and then overall exam and evaluation of my health. If they feel I'm trending down-ward they recommend hospitalization.

It's discouraging to know you will be spending two weeks or more stuck in a hospital room, but I have no other option.

I'm admitted to the 10th floor and immediately my blood pressure, temperature and blood oxygen level is taken. Soon after that the PIC nurse specialist comes in and puts a jell of lidocream on the inside of my arm just above the elbow. An hour or so later she inserts my PIC line. This takes about 20 minutes. It is a very sterile procedure, so there's a lot of prep time involved. I am then wheeled down to another floor to get an X-ray of my chest and arm to make sure the PIC is properly placed. I go back to my room and a few hours later receive my first medicine through my PIC. The medications I receive, usually antibiotics Tobramycin (TOBI) and Ceftazidime (CEFTAZ) combat my persistent bacterial infections. They are given to me at intervals of two, three or four times a day, depending on the medication and the strength.

The dedicated staff meets in a conference room at Women and Children's Hospital of Buffalo to discuss patients, treatments and the busy week that lies ahead.

A respiratory therapy program is vital to my daily health and my routine. I receive inhaled medications regularly during my two week "tune up". This also includes the vest treatment or chest PT three to four times per day depending on your health status.

A successful application of the use of inhaled antibiotics is used for the treatment of Pseudomonas aeruginosa infections in patients with cystic fibrosis. Chronic endobronchial Pseudomonas aeruginosa infection with recurrent exacerbations is a common complication of cystic fibrosis as this bacteria and fungus colonize in the thick secretions that our lungs are not able to expel.

I think every cystic has a favorite nurse and respiratory therapist and my favorite respiratory therapist is a man named Joe. Joe works his ass off, he is professional and efficient and is a great human being. He has become a good friend and when you are in this difficult situation sometimes you need a good friend, sometimes you need a Joe. He was one of those people I can't thank enough.

Occasionally I had blood drawn and a urine sample taken but for the most part it was a daily routine of antibiotics, lung therapy and crappy meals. After two weeks hopefully you were healthy enough to walk out the door. Sometimes that was the case, sometimes it wasn't, but one thing is for sure, it wasn't for the lack of effort from the dedicated professional people on the 10th floor at Women's and Children's Hospital, in Buffalo, NY.

Same Old, Same Old   March, 2004

Went into the hospital again. Same thing, same routine. FEV1 at 32%, down from 42%, FVC at 65%, down from 78%. This is a precautionary measure, a classic two week "tune up". I left the hospital with FEV1 38%, FVC 85%. I'll be back!!!

My sisters Candy and Holly call me often to see how I'm doing. I usually get the question "How are you doing"? or "How have you been feeling"? and I always reply the same way. "Fine" or "OK" are my usual responses. Then I'll always get the same thing back. "I'll bet." or "I'm sure" with the next question, "Really, how are you"? I never know what to tell them. Am I supposed to say that really I can't breathe worth a damn, or that I'm on oxygen at this very moment or that I coughed so hard for the last 10 minutes it completed exhausted me. I positively could not. There's nothing that they or anyone else could possibly do about it and I don't want to put them in the position of saying, "Oh, that's not good" or "Is there anything I can do for you"? As much as I appreciate my sisters calling me and asking me how things are going, there was not much I could say except the usual "OK" or "Good" or "Fine".
But I do appreciate you calling and thanks for caring!

Talk of Transplant   December, 2004

The last several visits to the Lung Clinic have been stressful ones. It's gotten to be tough enough just going in for clinic visits and learning the health of your body and lungs in particular, it's hardly ever good, but these last ones have been peppered with talk of transplantation. CF lung transplantation is needed to treat end-stage lung disease when other treatment options are no longer effective. "Because of the risks involved, transplants usually are reserved for people who are likely to die of their lung disease within one to two years."[12] Look, this scares the living shit out of me. I really just want to get the hell out of there and go back to work or home and pretend this health issue doesn't exist, but I sit there politely on the examining table as my doctor talks about the potential outcome of this double lung transplant procedure. I have talked with my wife about the whole transplantation thing. It is nerve wracking having such a discussion with your wife about this serious step in our families life, but it's much more anxiety driven when I'm having the discussion while I'm holding my 4 year old daughter. I am reluctant and the hospital personnel know it, but they really play up its' benefits and downplay the actual seriousness of the whole thing. I have been listening to this talk for about a year now, and only recently I have been actually seriously listening. Obviously if they keep bringing it up it must be important right?

But now my wife and I have finally agreed to proceed with the transplantation process. The social worker and doctor have told me they are going to go through the formalities of submitting the request to my insurance company. And assuming the request is approved I will then find out which hospital our insurance will accept. My only two choices are the University of Pittsburgh Medical Center, where most of the Buffalo CF lung transplant patients have their procedures performed, or the Cleveland Clinic. Wish us luck, I think we may need some.

At some point after Mikaela was born, she was around four or five I believe, Deb and I had a private meeting with our CF specialist. We inquired about having another child and what we should expect from me regarding my future health. He said among other things that my last year before transplant will be hell and I should expect it to be that way. I had been discussing this transplant issue with my doctors for several visits now and thought that perhaps I was just a year or a year and a half out from transplant and thought gosh, this wasn't hell at all. Unless I suddenly got seriously ill I could definitely handle this "hell" of a last year or so.

Well, I eventually experienced the hell he was talking about. It took longer than a year, it was closer to five years, but it found me and he was right.

Our First Terrifying/Exciting Visit
August 26, 2005

It's my wife's and my 8th wedding anniversary. We have our first appointment with the Cleveland Clinic in Cleveland, Ohio. I am being evaluated for a double lung transplant. I am 48 years old. My daughter, Mikaela is five years old now. She was extremely excited as she was going to spend the next two days at her grandparents' home and she got to pack her own Disney Princesses suitcase. She has no clue what is happening with her daddy, for her it is an adventure to her grandparents. At five years old that's exactly what she should think of these next two days, for me it is much, much more.

My insurance will only allow me to have the transplant in Cleveland as opposed to Pittsburgh where most of the potential lung transplant patients from Buffalo go. At this point in my CF life I had no other options, as I was doing everything I could do to stay healthy and alive, and although I don't believe I'm at the point of transplant yet, my doctors in Buffalo know it is only a matter of time and want me to be ready when the time for transplant comes.

I really don't know what to expect, because really most of the doctors and PA's have either never been to Cleveland Clinic or have not spent much time there and don't really know what to tell me about the place, just that it is in Cleveland, it is highly regarded as a leading center for lung and heart transplants and well…it was the only place that would accept my insurance that was within approximately a 500 mile radius of Buffalo.

As we drive on the I-90 Thruway toward Cleveland I honestly feel sick to my stomach. I know my life will be changed by this visit. I will either be accepted into their lung transplant program in which case at some point in the near future I will be transplanted and could potentially live a much more normal, happier life or I will be denied and will go home to slowly die like so many before me have in this situation. This is a time I have been hoping for and dreading too. It is a case of life or death, and it is not a story in a book or movie, it is my life. I am on the emotional edge now as we navigate our way into the Cleveland area, it seems anything my wife says pisses me off and there's nothing I can do about it. I don't know where the hell I'm going, my wife can't seem to read a damn map to save her life and damn it, it's my damn wedding anniversary.

My first appointment at Cleveland Clinic is at 7:30 am tomorrow, thankfully we arrived a day early to avoid exactly what's happening right now on tomorrows ride into the City of Cleveland. Finally we arrive at our hotel in Solon, Ohio which is a good 45 minutes east of the hospital.

Tomorrow we'll have to leave extremely early to find our way to the hospital, the rush hour traffic I'm sure will be bad. We have a full day tomorrow and it starts at 7:30 am. I can't relax now, I'm too wound up and anxious. What will happen, who will I see, what will they say, will they perform any tests that I am not expecting, (I hate that). I couldn't sleep, even with the Clonazepam I have been taking to calm my overall anxiety that I have had these past few years. Will my family be OK should I die? Will I eventually lose my job of almost 20 years if I get too sick? How will my house be paid off? Stuff like that haunts me.

Deb and I got up early the next morning and left for our first appointment. I am already exhausted, anxious, nervous and just down-right scared to death. We arrived at the hospital a little late, the morning traffic here in Cleveland is bad, we were slightly lost, but finally we have parked in one of the many multi-level parking lots around the hospital and entered onto the second floor at the end of what is called the Skyway which is a long walkway between two main buildings of the hospital. The Skyway goes over E. 100th Street and is also an entrance to the InterContinental Hotel. We enter the Crile Building, the bustling signature building of the Cleveland Clinic. The "Crile Building is the home of The Cleveland Clinic's busy outpatient services. The 12 stories contain the doctors' offices where patients make same-day visits for nearly every disorder of the body in every medical specialty. Some same-day surgeries, rehabilitation, and other services are offered here. The Crile Building has a soaring lobby, and two dining facilities, the Founders' Room and Au Bon Pain. It is named after George Crile, one of the founders of the Cleveland Clinic."[17]

Crile Building, Cleveland Clinic

My appointment schedule is full.

7:30 am I have a chest X-ray. No problem with that.

8:00 am I have a CAT scan. I'm injected with a dye from an IV in my hand, feel like I might have to pee which is common , experience the metallic taste in my mouth, all the usual feelings of a CAT scan of this type and then on to the Transplant Center at the financial counselor who reviews my health insurance and our personal financial situation.

Portable Pulse Oximeter

On to PFT's at 10 am. Damn, I hate PFT's. I'm given the full set, including the Body Box- also known as asplethysmography, which is done while sitting in an enclosed clear chamber while asked to perform a series of very small panting breaths. This is the most accurate way to measure lung volumes. Then I'm asked to do something I have never done. It is called the 6 minute walk. It measures the distance I can walk in six minutes and how much my blood is desaturating with a fingertip Pulse Oximeter. I walk 1,265 feet and I desat to 90%. Not bad I think.

11:30 am I meet with the first doctor at Cleveland Clinic. Dr. Marie Budev walks in to the examining room and greets me with a cheerful smile and handshake. She is a small, pretty young woman who I soon discover is not only upbeat but is brilliant.

Dr. Budev, my wife and I discuss why I'm there including my medical history, the results of my PFT's and six minute walk test and my overall attitude toward transplantation. At times she is very blunt and honestly she scares me with some statistics she throws at me. She asks me point blank if I am mentally and emotional prepared for such a major surgery. She believes I am healthy enough to have the surgery which in my mind is a relief. She asks me if I have any questions, which at the time I didn't simply because my head was swimming in facts, statistics and overall anxiety.

1:00 pm I meet with the social worker, then it's lunch. We go to the Founders' Room dining hall. We don't say much or eat much as I think we are both absorbing the gravity of the last few appointments. Our heads are swimming with emotions. This is heavy stuff, it's a lot to absorb and I know my head is reeling. The reality of it all is sinking in.

3:30 pm I meet with the doctor from infectious disease. The term *infectivity* describes the ability of an organism to enter, survive and multiply in the host. The host is me, the organism are the fungus and bacteria that live inside my lungs, which is slowing destroying them.

4:45 pm is my last appointment of the day and it's for blood work. I am amazed how much they take from me. I think it was around 10-12 vials. They sucked me almost dry. You know you're in trouble when they ask you to sit for a minute or two when they are finished and then tell you to stand up slowly.

My day of tests is complete.

It's about 6 pm now, and although I am still anxious I can at least relax. We have decided to stay until tomorrow and head back home well rested. We are anxious to see our daughter and once again enjoy the comfort and sanity of home.

That evening we drive over to a casual sit down restaurant which was too packed for us to wait. We moved on to another but the wait again was 30 minutes.

I wasn't in the mood to stand around in a crowd of people for thirty minutes. We ended up at KFC, ugh, but hey it wasn't crowded and then we went and saw a movie. It was a comedy, *The 40 Year Old Virgin* was playing, starring a relative new comer to the big screen and small screen, Steve Carell. I remember being distracted during the movie, my mind was on the day's events and all the information I was verbally given along with all the pamphlets, brochures and papers about the process of lung transplantation.

  The next day we headed back to Buffalo, and so this ended my first appointment at the Cleveland Clinic. I still don't know if this trip was a relief or a disappointment for me. I just know that I am worried about the future of my family.

A First for Everything   October, 2005

I am having my first colonoscopy at 48 years old. I am also nervous as hell. I have gotten a lot of advice from others who have already gone through this. Almost to a person they tell me that the preparation is worse than the procedure. I am not allowed to eat anything the day before the procedure. Although I don't eat a lot anyway, it's still an odd feeling. "The goal of the colonoscopy prep is to eliminate all fecal matter (stool) from the colon so that the physician conducting the colonoscopy will have a clear view of the intestinal wall. There are several ways to achieve this, and some doctors will have their own unique methods that work best for them."[11] I took a prescription of 255 grams of Miralax with Gatorade followed by 4 Bisacodyl tablets with water.

The amount of this medication and the amount I have to drink is ridiculous. It does however achieve its' goal of clearing me out. My procedure is completed without incident. Without incident means I don't remember a thing and I am good to go in "there". Thankfully that's over.

It's A Number's Game   July, 2006

Back in WCHOB again. FEV1 at 25%, FVC at 69%. I see a trend here. I took a nighttime oxygen saturation test. Nocturnal oximetry has found to be very low, in the 60's. I'm now on nighttime oxygen, 2L during sleep. I was waking up feeling crappy and it took me until maybe noon to start to feel myself again. Apparently it's because my body isn't getting enough oxygen during the nighttime hours. It's basically oxygen deprivation. Since I have been on nighttime oxygen I have been feeling much better.

Cleveland Visit   October, 6, 2006

This visit is about bone density and osteoporosis. Yes, it's true, I am a 49 year old male with mild osteoporosis. It is not uncommon for a person with cystic fibrosis to be at higher risk of developing osteoporosis, a dangerous thinning of bones. This may be linked to the body's inability to absorb vitamin D, which helps build strong bones. I have been taking Fosamax for stronger bone density for probably close to 5 years. I have had numerous body density tests (dexa scans) to watch my overall bone health. This visit I am instructed to increase my Vitamin D intake to 50,000 units twice a week.

Cleveland Visit   November 4, 2006

On the 4th of this month I had an appointment in Cleveland. I am doing my routine lab work (blood), always a chest X-Ray and PFT's then another CAT scan. I again meet with the doctor from infectious disease and they decide to give me two shots, one for pneumonia and the other for tetanus. Since I had no proof I had received a booster shot for tetanus in the last ten years I got a shot. I then go on to my final appointments with the nurse, pre-transplant coordinator and the doctor.

I'm done at 4:30 pm at which time Deb and I jump into our car, cross our fingers for the always exciting three hour drive home along Lake Erie and the infamous "lake effect" snow that impacts Erie, PA to Buffalo, NY. Although it's still early in the winter season for a large amount of snow to fall, you just never know and a lake storm is always a possibility. Wish us luck.

Down But Not Out – Feeling Sooo Bad
All of December, 2006

This illness is not one for the weak. You have to fight and fight like hell to not let it beat you down. You cannot win this war, but you can win some battles, and those victories are fulfilling. You can drag yourself into that hospital, or be wheeled in, or carried in, but if you can walk out, even it you're just a little better than when you walked in, then you are the temporary victor. You know you will be back, and you know you will probably crawl in again, but you have to fight, fight damn it, losing isn't an option you can accept.

In December of 2006 I got sick. Usually my illness was something I kept to myself and my battle was inward. No one knew how bad it was, although my wife had a pretty good idea, however even she was never completely aware of the struggle I went through. It truly was a feeling that only I could understand and trying to describe it would not do it justice. Usually I made as big an attempt to act as normal as possible, but this time was different. This was bad. When people at work told me I looked bad, I thought to myself, "well, if your lungs were only working at 25% of capacity, then yes you'd look bad too", but I would only smile and say, "yes I know, I am not feeling well". I would measure how I felt on any day by the elevator test. I parked my car at the back of the building where I worked. It was not a long walk to the front and into the front doors, through the vestibule and to reception area where the elevators were. I would park, my name plate assured of my designated spot, suck in some oxygen, get out of my car and stand there for just a second, maybe fumble with my key, or adjust my bag in my hand, this gave me time to catch my breath and go for it, and I did. I rarely passed anyone on my walk to the front of the building, which was good, talking and walking made for a disastrous result.

The front doors were rather heavy and it made for added stress on my body, then I'd walk through the vestibule and continue through to the reception area and to the elevators. STOP AND BREATH. If the receptionist said good morning, I would either be able to say good morning or say nothing. If I could say something I was having a decent day so far, if I could not catch my breath to speak, well the elevators would always provide me with the necessary four floors I needed to suck in as much oxygen as I could to catch my breath. That was my elevator test. Although everyday was a struggle some days were obviously better than others.

That last day of work was a struggle. I knew I was sick, but it seemed worse than usual, and to top it off I got a call from my daughter's elementary school to pick her up as she also was sick in the nurses' office. I pushed my illness to the back of my mind and went to pick my daughter up. There was no way I was going to be able to park in the school parking lot and walk that 200 feet, so I pulled right up as close to the door as possible and left the motor running. I barely made it into the nurse's office, thankfully it is very near the front entrance to the school. There I was able to catch my breath, talk as little as possible to the nurse and walk out to the car with my daughter in tow on willpower alone. We left the school for home; my daughter and I, both sick. Thank g-d it was Friday.

I called up Dr. Cronin that Friday evening at his home, his phone number; crazy him, was not unlisted. My doctor was a cystic fibrosis specialist and he was good. His wife answered and she sounded upset. Obviously a few too many patients have had the same bright idea as I did and she was most likely tired of it. I felt extremely uncomfortable by this time as Dr. Cronin didn't seem too happy to be bothered either, and after profusely apologizing to him, he told me to take Tamiflu and see how I felt. He told me to contact him on Monday morning. If things got worse, go to the emergency room.

I thought about that advice a lot on Friday night. With my disease, the only place I could go and be properly treated was Women and Children's Hospital. I did not want to see myself waiting in that emergency room though. I made it through the week-end at home. It was brutal. I called the Lung Center on Monday morning.

I was goin' in for a "tune up" and it probably was the first time ever that I was happy to do it. It was just prior to the winter holiday break, but I believed I would be home for the Hanukkah, Christmas holiday.

The pulmonary department calls it a "tune up" which means approximately two weeks of antibiotics through a PICC line and then 2 weeks of oral antibiotics at home, with a follow-up visit at the lung clinic to see where you are, according to your given baseline. Usually after about a week or two I would be feeling better, but this was not happening at this "tune up" and I expressed my dismay to anyone who would listen. My doctor was extremely busy and I did not see him until the second week I was in. I was not happy and I told him, as a matter of fact, I told him I felt he was missing something as this was unusual for me. I had seen no progress in nearly two weeks and this was not like me. I remember my doctor leaning against a night stand in my room and saying to me "I think I can keep you alive for about one more year". I heard the words but did not believe them, I knew he was missing something and once they discovered it, I would get to my former baseline. I was exhausted and was still always coughing and it was difficult to get any sleep and still couldn't breathe; they needed to discover what was going on.

My wife and daughter came in one evening to visit. My daughter looked so beautiful, she was wearing a dress as she and my wife were going to an event at our temple downtown. I took off my oxygen and hung my cannula off my ear. It was extremely difficult without my oxygen on, but I didn't want her see me looking so sick and venerable. She had seen me with my oxygen on before, but only at night just at her bedtime and initially I would attempt to hide it from her completely but sometimes she would unexpectedly come into our bedroom to say goodnight (this is when I still slept in our bed) and see me with it. She was always very understanding of my issues and did not question my unusual circumstances, although I'm sure she wondered what it all meant. Apparently she had never seen the cannula hanging over my ear before and thought it was somehow attached to the side of my head. About a year later she told me this and I had to laugh, because she never question- ed it or stared at it during their visit.

It's amazing what is going on in my daughters mind about her kooky father. It often bothered me what she thought about me and my ability to do, or not be able to do almost everything.

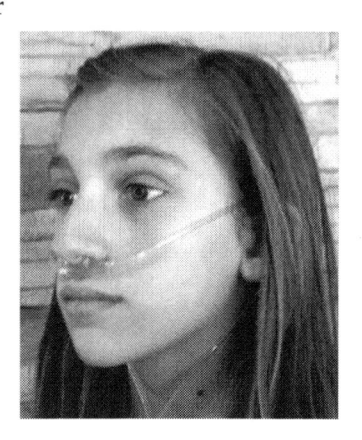

My daughter demonstrates the proper use of an oxygen providing cannula.

She would always make gifts for me at school, you know, Father's Day magnets, holiday cards, pictures drawn of me, which I still have hanging on my wall and without fail she told me I was the best father ever and she loved me so much. It always made me cry to read that and as I type this now it still does, because I wondered how she could possibly think this of me? I was not by any means your typical father. Often times I felt that I was cheating her out of many father/daughter moments, yet she seemed to love me just the same.
I am always proud of her because of that, she truly is a gift

from G-d to a truly unworthy dad.

Anyway my doctor finally got me to have a CAT scan on my upper torso and lungs, previously I had just an X-Ray. I remember I could barely make it onto the long CAT scan bed and lying down flat on my back was a feeling like nothing you have ever experienced. Imagine having a 200lb. bag of sand lying across your chest and only being able to breathe through a straw. I had to lie this way as I made my way through the CAT scan machine. G-d it was tough, I couldn't wait to get upright and back into a wheelchair.

Nights were by far the toughest. I could not lie flat, I could not recline, I could not sleep on my stomach. The only way to sleep was sitting up in a chair; but the coughing, the coughing, if only I could stop the coughing. I was exhausted from the coughing and needed to sleep but the coughing would also keep me awake. I could hardly breathe even with the constant oxygen and struggling to breath expended my energy further still.

This disease was beating the shit out of me and in the still of the night, when you mind and spirit are most fragile, I believed I might just die. It was almost more than I could stand, almost more than I could tolerate, almost more than me... Almost.

Down But Not Out - The Correct Diagnosis
All of December, 2006

Well, they found that I had pneumonia and *finally* it made sense. And they finally started to treat this illness using different antibiotics and medications.

Approximately one week into my new medication regiment I started to feel better. I was in the hospital for a whole month in December and into January. I came out for Christmas day and was permitted to go to my sisters for a few hours that evening, celebrate Christmas with my family and then went back into the hospital to be a patient once again. Kind of a "pass" to normal life for just a few hours. Believe me, going back to that hospital after being out was one difficult task to bear and I had to force myself to do it.

When I had my CAT scan the physicians also found a blockage in my lower intestines. One evening my nurse came into my room and said to me, out of the blue that I was scheduled for a procedure to have the blockage removed immediately. I was not at all thrilled at this news. I asked him to get in contact with my doctor and please explain to me what was going on. When Dr. Cronin did finally get back to me, he told me to relax and have it done, if I didn't I would have a bowel obstruction eventually.

What a shitty, and I use that term literally, procedure. The doctor had me lie down and basically gave me an atomic anemia. I had a hose up my anus for a good hour. He cleared my obstruction and I finally climbed off that steel bed with shit all over my backside. As soon as that fun fest was over I was able to clean up enough to go back to my room and take a shower.

I was still on constant oxygen and used it always, even while taking a shower, so that meant taking the portable with me to the shower, which was fine except I needed to get a respiratory therapist to fill a portable tank and of course that takes a bit of time as they need to fill it on a different floor, so I sat in my own doo-doo for a while. To be quite honest, the smell is OK for me as I had my sinuses scraped when I was in college and it basically took away all my ability to smell almost anything and that includes my own bowel movements. It was just the feeling on my skin that gave me the hebe jebies.

My nurse came in after I was cleaned up and asked me how it was doing. When I told him he gave me the scrunched up face look. *He is a nurse*, he shouldn't be giving me the scrunched up face look! But he probably had a good idea what was involved and he too was a little grossed out by it all.

At the end of that month-long stay I walked out feeling darn good, my PFT's were not only base line, they were a better baseline. My doctor said they were better then they had ever been! I was off daytime oxygen once again and used it only at nighttime as usual.

Of course, those great PFT's didn't last and within two months my numbers were back down to the "you need a tune-up" levels. After all, you don't "get better" with this disease, you just try to "not get worse".

Colonoscopy #2 January, 2007

There's no lung transplant without a colonoscopy. I have found the most difficult part of a colonoscopy is the preparation. The actual procedure isn't bad at all. You are virtually out and unaware for the whole procedure although it's called a "twilight" procedure which means you're technically awake. I had a few polyps that were removed. Nonmalignant. Done.

The Cleveland doctors had wanted me to have a colonoscopy every two years and one just prior to my transplant as I was getting on to three years. I remember my doctor during one of my last Cleveland visits before my transplant reviewing my chart and noting the lapse of their required two years.

Soon after that Cleveland visit, I was sent a letter that listed the tests I needed to have performed prior to transplant and sure enough, the colonoscopy was on there. I made a call to the pre-transplant coordinator and was able to persuade them to eliminate that procedure from the list. I was worried I could not go through the stress of it all. At that point in my existence, I was having real troubles dressing, walking, breathing, living.

My Peg   March, 2007

For quite some time my doctor has been suggesting I receive a PEG line. A PEG (Percutaneous endoscopic gastrostomy) is an endoscopic medical procedure in which a tube (PEG tube) is passed into a patient's stomach through the abdominal wall, most commonly to provide a means of feeding when oral intake is not adequate.

My CF doctor has felt it will improve my overall health and nutritional needs which have been sorely lacking for some time. I had resisted the idea but now I am grudgingly getting it. I am obviously very nervous, the pain of the procedure does not scare me as much as a foreign object protruding out of my stomach. Honestly, I don't know what to expect. I do know it is not uncommon for a person of any age with CF to have a PEG line. Most of us have nutritional issues that have to be addressed.

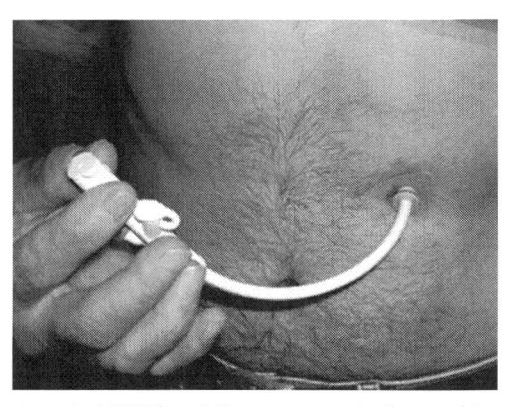

A typical PEG line. Mine was very similar to this one. The line being held is attached to the "button" at the stomach. The piece in this man's hand connects to a feeding tube that runs from a hanging bag. The hanging bag is filled with a high calorie nutritional supplement that is fed directly into your stomach during sleep. Some fun!

My sister Holly accompanied me for moral support, an ear for post procedure follow-up and a safe drive home. The procedure takes only a few minutes, probably less than 20 minutes. "The Gauderer-Ponsky technique, which I had, involves performing a gastroscopy to evaluate the anatomy of the stomach. The anterior stomach wall is identified and techniques are used to ensure that there is no organ between the wall and the skin. The light emitted from the endoscope within the stomach can be seen through the abdominal wall. An angiocath is used to puncture the abdominal wall through a small incision, and a soft guidewire is inserted through this and pulled out of the mouth. The feeding tube is attached to the guidewire and pulled through the mouth, esophagus, stomach, and out of the incision. A bumper in the stomach keeps the PEG from getting pulled out through the incision and a spacer on the outside keeps the PEG from going into the stomach. "[10]

Damn, one more thing to worry about but now I will be getting the calories and nutritional supplements that I have been lacking these past few years of not eating. It also frees me up from the laborious task of eating itself, which I found to be so tiring.

Hospital Birthday #1   May, 16 2007

I've turned 50 years old and spent my birthday in the hospital. My daughter is going to be celebrating her 7th birthday on the 24th of May. I hope I make it out of here for her birthday celebration. My FEV1 is 18% and my FVC is 62%. Is my birthday a cause for celebration or concern? It is part of my life.

Our biggest trade show of the year usually puts me here. I get tired out, my immune system breaks down, I get sick and end up in the hospital. Fortunately the show is done and the leasing agents have gone on their way to sunny Las Vegas.

You take simple things like walking for granted. DON'T. When you can't walk, whether it's from a stroke or a broken leg or a bum pair of lungs, getting around is complicated. It's a form of independence and you really don't know its' importance until it's gone. It was essentially gone for me. I could still get around, although it was slow, measured and not very far. At home it was often with oxygen and it was fatiguing. I spend a lot of time sitting in a chair or on a bed and praying for a quick, easy trip to the bathroom or to the kitchen or the car. It's almost never that easy. It takes all my energy even with oxygen and I am exhausted when I get there, whether it is 30 feet or just a few feet. Although I am still working and attending as many social functions, ie: birthdays, holidays, family dinners as always, it is getting extremely difficult and taxing on my body. It should be easy to go to work or over to my sisters or in-laws for dinner, right? It is not. I can't wait to get home once again and back on my oxygen.

May 24th, 2007 – I didn't make it out of the hospital for my daughter's birthday, but my mom picked me up at the hospital and drove me to the birthday party she had with her friends at a local craft store. We then had a quick celebration at home and I was driven back to the hospital to finish my stay. I tried my best to be out the hospital in time, but it just didn't work out. Next year I will make it up to her and be there for her big day.

A Typical Working Day   September 2007

I wake up at 5:50 am and immediately take a shower. My routine was to always take a shower before my family's day had begun. I can feel the tightness in my chest. I don't have to cough yet, and if I did it would be a dry cough. Get out of the shower and get on my vest. The vest is actually a machine that blows air through two long (5 ft.) tubes in a rapid beat. You can adjust the speed of the beat and the range of the beat. The two tubes are attached to a vest. It's actually a nylon vest that snaps on with large plastic clips and contains two holes in the front for the tubes to attach. When running and attached the vest fills with air and vibrates in a patterned beat. The object of the patterned vibrating beat is to shake your lungs (and whole body really) and loosen the thick secretions in your lungs. You're on the vest for ½ hour in the morning and also do an albuterol inhaler and Tobi inhaler to open up your airways and to add an antibiotic while they are open.

After the half-hour is over I wake up my wife, Deborah so she can take a shower and then wake up my daughter to get ready for school. I always value these mornings of being able to wake Mikaela up. While my wife would rather get ready to start her day, I enjoy waking our daughter up.

I look forward to it and view it as an opportunity. I want Mikaela to understand I am part of her morning routine and that she can count on me each day.

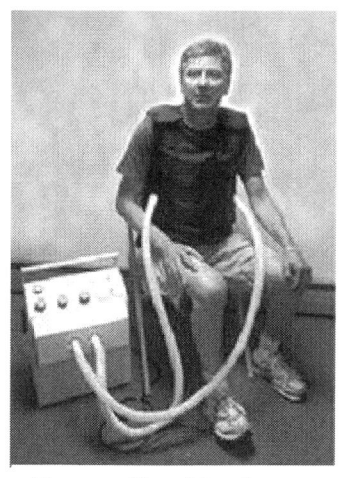

Me on my Vest. Many hours were spent like this.

While I am getting my daughter ready for school which means breakfast, dressing, washing, my wife is getting ready too and one of us takes her to the morning program at her school. Since we both have to be at work early the morning program is a good solution for Deb and I. Mikaela's generally bored at it as you have to occupy yourself for about an hour and they offer no structured activities, but we have no other option at this point.

During this morning prepping period I usually have my coughing time, where I clear up all the thick secretions that have accumulated in my lungs while I slept. The coughing is fierce and often times after just a few coughs I get the dry heaves or perhaps throw-up, hopefully into a sink or toilet although I have thrown up on the floor. The dry heaves or throwing up would occur every morning with few exceptions. What came out of my stomach also came out of my lungs. Large amounts of yellow or green secretions is not unusual if you are a CF'er.

I once threw up after dropping off my daughter off at school right in my car on the way to work. It went everywhere, I mean everywhere inside the front seats of my car. I had to go back home, hose off my car floor mats, clean my seats, steering wheel, dashboard and change my clothes. This was not a fun experience and I make every effort to throw up at home before I left for the day, although often times it would happen on my way to work in the fast lane on the expressway. If you've ever thrown up in your mouth and had to swallow it again you know this terrible feeling. I know it sounds disgusting but this is an aspect of having cystic fibrosis that if I didn't mention I would not be letting you know how tough this disease can be on the body. I lived with this issue every day for at least three years. There was never a week off or even a few days off, it was an everyday speed bump in my busy and full day.

I would work the whole day, the job, although I loved it,

was extremely stressful. Sometimes if my day was more difficult I would try not to walk too far or too fast as I would tire out too early. That did not however change my time I left work for the day and around 6pm I would go home.

Often times on the way home I would make a work related stop. Those stops were usually to a printer, a large format copier company, to take photographs of our properties or to our own warehouse to pick or drop off work related items.

I would get home usually between 6:30 -7 pm, change out of my work clothes and almost immediately have dinner with my family, often times just nibbling at it as my appetite was extremely poor, sometimes I was too tired to expend energy eating at all.

Before bed, I would do the whole vest thing over again, usually with a different inhaled drug. At bedtime I would set-up my night time nutritional feeds to the button (PEG) in my stomach, put on my O2 (one of my favorite times of the day because I was getting the oxygen my body craved and needed) and sleep in a chair with my feet up because they were swollen from the excess fluid in them. At about 3:30 am my feeds would be complete, I would unhook myself, clean myself and the tubing up and go to bed until 5:50 am. It was an exhausting and busy routine but I had to do it and skipping it would just shorten my days and my "quality of life".

The Fight of Your Life

CF consumes your life, it's a daily fight, yet many of us CF'ers live our lives as normal as possible and for many normal is doing their routine every day. Vest, inhaled medications, oral medications, then your "normal" day, vest, PEG supplements, start over again. Many CF'ers do more, some do less. You can't let the disease get the upper hand, although in many ways it already has, but you must work to keep the saneness and normalness of your life into each day.

It has become a routine for me to get as much oxygen as I can before leaving my home to go on an appointment or to a social event. I'll typically be sitting in a chair waiting for the final countdown. "Are you ready to go?", my wife will ask. "Yes, just give me a few more minutes", I'll reply. And she will wait. Reluctantly and always too soon I will take off my cannula, turn my O2 off and head out the door. Perhaps it's to my sisters or mothers for a family function or a neighbor's house for a party. I always have the same feeling, and it's the feeling of anxious anticipation to get back home and get that oxygen back on. The discomfort of no O2 combined with the effort of acting as though everything is normal and nothing is wrong with me is exhausting. Sometimes it will be hours before I get my relief, but sometimes if it's a neighbor's home I will be able to walk back home (or drive if I can't walk the distance) after maybe a half hour or so and get my "fix" of O2. Then reluctantly I will head back to the party and presto, everything seems fine to others. This is an unfortunate reality of having CF. There is almost never a comfortable moment without oxygen now, even if it appears other-wise. It is truly something I rely on to make life easier.

I will never forget going to the lung clinic for a scheduled appointment, I was still working downtown at that time.

I had my appointment, met with my doctor, respiratory therapist, dietician and the other various people that watch and guide your progress and I was checking out and making my co-pay. Through a door was a man, probably in his 30's sitting in a wheel chair in the hallway where the CF exam rooms are located. He looked at me with sad, unhappy eyes. I knew he was being admitted to the 10th floor of WCHOB, no doubt for a two week "tune-up". I thought to myself, "He looks terrible, thankfully I am not like him". I left and went to work. I tried to put him out of my mind, but never forgot him, especially when eventually I became him.

I guarantee you nobody at work ever knew the problems I have or the ridiculous routine I go through each day. They often said I coughed a lot or commented that I was too thin and underweight. It was too hard to explain why I was this way. This is my secret that I must keep to myself. It's nobody's business and I liked to keep it that way.

For quite a few years even my in-laws did not know about my disease, it can be kept a secret if your health is still manageable and you try hard to hide it. The first time I was admitted to the hospital for a "tune-up" we told my in-laws I was out of town on business and would be gone for a week. It was the wrong thing to do, I know that now, but at the time I was very reticent to have anyone know about my illness, it was very personal issue to me and a select few.

I remember many times walking throughout our house, it is a ranch, and wondering how I was going to feel when I got to where I was going. Or even if I was going to make it there without having to stop and take a breather, if you want to call it that, it was more like a gasper. I was actually always sucking in air and gasping to breathe. It's an odd feeling living in a world where you cannot breathe. It is unexplainable and hard to comprehend. The people around me don't understand or get it, and I wouldn't expect them to. You look OK for the most part, although I had been told my coloring was not great, but otherwise you look fine. Fine is *not* what you feel. I remember Billy Crystal on *Saturday Night Live* saying "It's better to look good than to feel good", and that is what I always felt.

Just prior to my transplant when I was feeling exceptionally bad or tired it was always a struggle to eat. It actually took more energy to eat than it was worth and sometimes I would just skip dinner and have a high calorie drink instead. I felt it was better to conserve my energy and drink a high calorie supplement than to eat just a small amount of food and expend too much energy. To me it was wasted energy and it was something that needed to be conserved at all costs. Then during the nighttime hours I hooked on my nutritional feeds for added calories. I always wanted the people around me, especially my daughter to believe I was better than I was. It was not worth the worry, there was nothing that could be done about it and I didn't want to talk about it. So I went about my life, pushing through as best I could, ignoring the disease that was destroying me and my lungs.

Heart Catheterization #1   January 8th, 2007

I'm having my first heart catheterization. This is just one of the many tests I've had and probably will have to assure my transplantation comes with no surprises. I have never had this test performed before. It's being performed at Buffalo General Hospital. Local anesthetic is injected into my skin in the right groin to numb the area. "In some centers access to the coronary arteries is made via the right radial or brachial artery (hand or arm), but the majority of cases are still done from the groin region. A puncture is then made with a needle in either the femoral artery in the groin or the radial artery in the wrist, (Seldinger technique), before a guidewire is inserted into the arterial puncture. A plastic sheath (with a stiffer plastic introducer inside it) is then threaded over the wire and pushed into the artery. The wire is then removed and the side-port of the sheath is aspirated to ensure arterial blood flows back. It is then flushed with saline. This arterial sheath, with a bleedback prevention valve, acts as a conduit into the artery for the duration of the procedure. Catheters are inserted using a guidewire and moved towards the heart. Once in position above the aortic valve the guidewire is then removed. The catheter is then engaged with the origin of the coronary artery (either left main stem or right coronary artery) and X-Ray opaque iodine-based contrast is injected to make the coronary vessels show up on the x-ray fluoroscopy image. A cardiac catheterization is a general term for a group of procedures that are performed using this method, such as coronary angiography, as well as left ventrical angiography and aortography"[8] which is what was performed on me.

The procedure performed today is necessary to evaluate my hearts overall health. After the procedure I have to lie perfectly still while a heavy bag is laid on the area where the procedure was performed. The femoral artery must coagulate and close up so I can stand up and be discharged. I honestly can't remember how the artery was closed, I remember the heaviness on my leg and groin area, and seem to remember a nurse telling me they were using a weighted bag, but they may have used a clamp or wrapped the leg too. I could not see what they were doing and did not ask. It takes almost two hours before they take the weight off the area where they made the incision. After the nurses are certain I can stand without any major complications, they let me get dressed.

   I know the transplant team will reject me if my heart is not suitable to withstand the transplant and post-transplant stress. Thankfully my heart, like both my parents (thank you mom and dad) is strong and capable to withstand the transplant surgery.

How Could This Happen   December 7, 2007

My sister Holly came to see me today. I was at the sink in our kitchen, my wife and daughter were not yet home from school. It's the start of the week-end. She looked anxious and serious. She had something bad to tell me, I could tell. She said she had something important to tell me and it wasn't good news. My first instinct was something had happened to my mom, then I thought of my father.

She told me Brad had died. I was stunned. You know when you're so caught off guard that you can't think clearly, can't speak, don't know how to react at such shocking news. That's how I feel. Brad is my best friend. I have known him since elementary school. He was one of those guys that just stuck with you. Brad was the kind of person who had many best friends, and was the best man at many weddings. He was my best man at my wedding. A person like Brad is unique because he invests so much of himself into his friends and they are the ones who benefit greatly from it. It didn't matter if you didn't see him for a month or you saw him every day. He just stuck with you. A friend's friend. We always called each other on our birthdays. It was a tradition. He let me have it one year that I forgot. I deserved it, because he would not have forgotten. That's the kind of friend he was. He just stuck with you. He always came to the hospital to visit me during my "tune-ups". Now he was gone. Forever. Brad died of an apparent heart attack. He was only 50 years old. I was relying on him to help Deb and I get through these next few difficult years. I was relying on him to be there for me. How could this happen? How could I, with these lungs that were almost useless be living and he be dead? I am always amazed by such things. It makes no sense, yet it happens every day. He will always be my best friend.

The three Amigos. My best friends, Brad on the left and Kevin in the middle. I'm on the right. Believe it or not, plaid was a cool fashion statement in the '70's.

A "Lake Effect" Adventure   February 6, 2008

I have yet another appointment in Cleveland. My sister Holly who is educated in and works in the field of medicine has been asking me if she could come along and see for herself what a visit to Cleveland Clinic was like for me. She deals with doctors on a daily basis at a Buffalo hospital as a doctor liaison. Don't ask me what that is. But apparently I am not good enough at explaining to her just what happens and my liaison skills stink. We leave on Monday afternoon and get to the beautiful Guest House around 5:00 pm. It's dark when we arrive, it gets dark so early now, it is February after all. We're over to the Clinic bright and early the next day. It's damn cold here in Cleveland, not unlike Buffalo. This morning it's probably in the 20's. I have blood work at 8:30 am, then on to Otolaryngology with Dr. Kominsky. At 10:30 am I have a CAT scan, then an X-Ray. I then meet with Dr. Avery who specializes among other things in transplantation and infectious disease. My sister listens intently, asks few questions. Then on to PFT's, the six minute walk and then my appointment with Dr. Budev. This is the part my sister has been waiting for. To meet my pre-transplant doctor and find out firsthand what they have to say about my present health, my status in the transplant process and generally what is said during a doctor's visit. Again she asks few questions, so maybe I wasn't such a bad liaison after all. We're done with the day, always exhausting for me around 4:30 pm. It has been snowing lightly throughout the day. Watching the snow fall outside the big wall of windows in the Crile Building makes for an anxious wait in between my appointments. What you really want to do is say screw it and get in the car and drive home, mostly because you know the longer you wait the worse it will probably get. When we do leave it is not snowing, and it does not start to really snow until we get into Pennsylvania, about one hour into the trip home. It snows rather steady but lightly throughout the most western part of Pennsylvania. It's been dark for literally the whole trip and the shit hits the fan just about 15 minutes past the New York State line. We have at least an hour to go. If you've ever driven in a white out you know the feeling of immense terror for your life and the life of the others in your automobile. I could not see anything, although I knew there had to be a car or truck in front of me somewhere. With the snow coming down hard and the wind blowing off Lake Erie we were caught in a classic "Lake Effect" storm. I think of pulling over and waiting it out, but decide against it as I really don't know where the road ends and the apron begins or how wide it even is. I really didn't want to go over the edge of an embankment and get stuck 10 or 20 feet down where no one could potentially see you. Should I get safely stopped on or near the apron of the Thruway I don't want someone to drive into the back of me either. Even at 10 or 15 miles an hour, that could be deadly so I kept on driving. Again, my sister doesn't say much, this time however for a totally different reason. It is tough enough driving without backseat advice and she knows it. I am now driving at approximately 10 miles per hour with my flashers on. Nobody's passing me and I was not gaining on anyone ahead. Crap, this sucks. My hands are holding onto the steering wheel so tight they hurt. I prayed to drive out of this band of whiteness and can't understand how much snow can possibly fall out of the sky so fast. Ten minutes pass and the constant whiteness has made me hyper alert yet exhausted. Nobody has said almost anything. Finally about 15 minutes in this nightmare it starts letting up, and by "letting up" I mean you can see the road now and make out up from down. After another five minutes it's snowing moderate to heavy which on most days is bad but at this point I'll gladly take. Less than ½ hour into our adventure it is basically over and is snowing rather lightly. I am never so glad to get back from Cleveland. I bet this made my sister think twice about making the trip to Cleveland again, at least in winter.

Hospital Birthday #2   May 16, 2008

I've turned 51 years old and again spent it in the hospital. It's another two to three week tune-up. Mother's Day which was just a few days ago was brutal. The last thing I wanted to do was, well, anything, but we had my in-law's over for a nice Mother's Day dinner. It was the right thing to do on Mother's Day but I was suffering big time. I did as I often do when we have anyone over. I go into the family room, kitchen or dining room, socialize a bit and then head into our bedroom, hook up the O2 and sit for five minutes to revive my body. I don't ever socialize with a cannula in my nose and my O2 on. Although my relatives are aware of my illness now, I still am not ready for them to see me in that venerable way. Maybe its' vanity or pride, but it's not an option…yet. After the five or so minutes of breathing in 99% pure oxygen which my body really needs I head back to my family and act as though life is normal. No problems! It's a difficult few hours but when my relatives have left I immediately put on the O2 and keep it on until, well… I keep it on.

On Monday morning I have my scheduled Clinic appointment and I'm prepared to start my hospital stay. Although I hate being in the hospital on my birthday, I know it will make me feel better. It is part of life, my life.

I will miss my daughter's birthday again damn it! She's having her party with friends at a bounce gym. Deb and I went to look at it three weeks ago. It has bounce houses, bounce slides and a bounce obstacle course. I will have a family member drive me to her party and after a few hours' drive me back to the hospital. I hate missing these opportunities with my daughter. What does she think of her dad missing her birthday again? I suppose I don't really want to even know the answer to that one.

This stay is not only on my birthday but before the ICSC show which the company I work for attends in Las Vegas. This makes getting everything accomplished for an error free show extremely problematic. It means knowing how much I can tolerate before I have to "give in" and I have been weighing this particular problem for quite a few weeks. I do complete my work for the show in time, but it's getting harder and harder.

Bad Months to be Me
May, (November and December too) 2008

I always seem to be in the hospital around May and November through December. I believe I'm in the hospital in May due to my work schedule. Benderson, the company I am employed at, has a trade show in mid-May every year. It is big, our biggest show of the year and takes place in Las Vegas. The show takes a huge amount of preparation and time and during the last couple weeks I am working on it constantly. I love my job, I really don't think my boss will ever understand how much I love it or how much it's hurting me. It's my fault for both of those. As always, I drop off my daughter at her morning program before school starts and head to work. I am having trouble making the walk from the car to the school cafeteria where the morning program is held and then back to my car. When I'm finally back in my car I am totally out of breath. Needless to say, I have a busy, busy day ahead of me and cannot possibly leave work until 6, 7 or maybe even later tonight.

This year I don't make it to the end. Well, that is to say I don't make it to the last Friday before the leasing agents leave for Las Vegas. Usually they fly out during the week-end or on the Monday morning of the show.

This year I end up in the hospital a week early. So files are forwarded to me by email and sent over on CD to complete. I fortunately have finished the bulk of the work. Last week I attempted to get all the large format graphics out for printing so I would have one less thing to worry about. I went into the hospital with about 95% of the work completed, but until the last leasing agent actually boards their plane, there still will be work to do.

When everything is done which is usually the week-end before the show and the leasing agents are finally leaving on their flights to Las Vegas with the show opening on that Monday morning I am physically spent. My body is burned out, my lungs are shot, my resistance to infection is gone and I am in the hospital. This year I just couldn't do it. I have been thinking of asking my employer if I can begin to work at home. They will not be thrilled, they believe you cannot possibly work as effective at home as in the office. We'll see what happens…

November and December are cold and flu season, I'm *always* sick then. Need I say more.

Feeling Crappy at New Year's
January 2, 2009

It's the start of a new year! We celebrated the imminent New Year with fresh lobster for dinner and champagne at midnight. Potato chips, soda pop, pretzels and beer were mixed in for good measure. Deb's brother David, his wife Donna and their children Joshua who is one year younger and Ava who is three years younger than Mikaela joined us to… "*should auld acquaintance be forgot, and never brought to mind*"?, whatever that means. Anyway, that's how we celebrated the last day of' 08 and the first of '09.

But today I have an appointment at the WCHOB lung clinic. We will see what happens as always. I am in a perpetual state of crappiness, if there is such a word.

My FVC is 64%, and my FEV1 is 23%. I am in the hospital every three to six months now like clockwork. I don't think I remember what good feels like anymore, and I don't think I know what leaving the hospital feeling good feels like anymore after my "tune ups". I think the "tune ups" are just trying to preserve my health so that I don't drop like a rotten apple off the transplant tree of life.

Heart Catheterization # 2   April 23, 2009

I'm having my second heart catheterization today at Millard Fillmore Gates Circle Hospital. It's been about a year and a half since my last one and Cleveland likes to keep up with the overall health of your body. If an important test hasn't been performed in a two year span they would like you to repeat it. They believe that is a long enough period to have gone by for your body to have experienced a possible dramatic health change. Gates is an excellent hospital with specialized programs that include world class neurological and stroke care services. The hospital has world renowned doctors, lifesaving procedures and state-of-the-art technology.

This is the hospital that former NFL player Kevin Everett of the Buffalo Bills was brought to when he sustained a spinal cord injury on the football field in September, 2007. Everett was infused with cold saline, inducing hypothermia within 15 minutes of his injury. By infusing patients with cold saline, doctors lower their core temperature. This slows down the body's responses to injury, which, in Everett's case, may have given doctors valuable time to decompress his spinal cord before more damage was done. Kevin Everett walks today. A testament to the skill and professionalism of these doctors.

Today is a tough day for me, but every day now it a tough day. I'm going to wear oxygen during this procedure; I can't bear to be without it at this point. The cath. procedure is going to be performed through the wrist this time. The last time it was through my groin. I like this way better as it seems less intrusive on my body. The procedure takes about an hour. I'm given the "it's a go" sign once again. Transplant here I come.

I've Made it This Far July 2, 2009

It's been about six months since I was in the hospital last. My FVC today is at 53% and my FEV1 is at 19%. I will go in once again for the "tune up" routine. I know I am not as bad off as many people with this disease but still, *this sucks!*

I am always optimistic that I will improve after these hospital "tune ups" and I will leave feeling better than ever but let me tell you…it's getting harder and harder. The last several hospital stays I haven't made much or any improvement and that's frustrating. I'm not complaining, I'm just saying. "Hey, what's the deal, this is how it works for those NOT listening. I get two, three, maybe four weeks of antibiotics and I feel better, I need to feel better".

It's true, I can't go on like this much longer, it's taken a toll on this old body and although I hate to admit it, maybe a new chance at life wouldn't be so bad. I made it this far, how could a transplant be that much worse than how I'm living now. If I make it through the surgery and still feel crappy, well then I'm pretty much even.

I end up in the hospital for just two weeks. My FVC is 61%, my FEV1 is 21% and I walk, definitely don't like the walking out part. I've said it before and I'll say it again, "I'll be back"!

Too Long and Too Tired   July 20, 2009

I'm fresh out of Women and Children's Hospital and off to Cleveland Clinic. I've been going every 2-3 months now for the last couple years or so. I guess they are waiting for that drop-off in health that is expected just prior to getting transplanted. I don't know if I've hit it yet but I'm sure they'll tell me when they believe I'm ready for the big one. Again we are in Cleveland a day early as my first appointment as always is at 7:30 or 8 am.

We have been staying at the Guest House which is run by the Cleveland Clinic. The Guest House is a hotel almost exclusively for patients or patients families to the Cleveland Clinic. The Guest House is convenient but that's it. It's old, poorly run and not inexpensive for what it offers. The ONLY upside to the hotel is its' proximity to Cleveland Clinic. Otherwise it offers almost no amenities or special services. It's located directly across the street from the hospital and a shuttle bus will pick us up at the hotel and drop us off right at the front entrance to the Crile Building. This is where I usually have my blood work done and always where I have my doctors' appointments.

My wife is wheeling me around the hospital now. I walk when I can, but only if it's not too far. Today my appointments are as follows: Blood work, X-Ray, CAT scan, Social Worker, PFT's, ENT, appointment with pre-transplant doctor, this appointment is with Dr. Minai, then finally Cardiothoracic. Dr. McCurry meets with us to go over the transplant procedures and to see how I'm generally doing. Dr. McCurry is the doctor assigned to my lung transplant surgery although I wonder how they would know that since donor lungs could be available at any time on any day. He is acutely aware of my heart health as well as my lung health. My day is over late but we head back to Buffalo. It's still light out and will be until we get into the Western New York area. It's a pleasure to travel in the summer. My wife as always, drives now. I know I'm close to transplant, although I never actually want to admit it to anyone. I can't do much at this point. I have had to let my pride take a back seat to my health.

My Typical Cleveland Appointment

When I first met the doctors in Cleveland they felt I was a good candidate for transplant, as I was relatively healthy for a CF adult, my heart was strong and although I had CF related diabetes, it was not terribly bad. Throughout the years I visited Cleveland every 2-4 or so months for tests and procedures.

A typical appointment which I have been having for the last five years went more or less like this:
8 am Blood work, sometimes as many as 15 vials were taken, sometimes as few as six.
8:30 am Chest X-ray. Usually in the basement of the Cleveland Clinic, although as with the blood work there are many places at the Clinic you could these tests done and sometimes I would have a chest X-Ray in the Crile Building or heart building or the blood work taken in the old, old original section of Cleveland Clinic, I think they simply call it the S Building or the Crile Building.. Sometimes I am scheduled for a CAT scan. This was always performed right after my chest X-Ray.
9 am PFT's UGH!! When you're sick with a lung disease, PFT's are the worst. They measure the capacity of your lungs, how much air you can suck in and how much air you can blow out. They're tough to do, you don't have any oxygen to begin with and then you're asked to blow as hard and as long as you can into a hard plastic tube attached to an apparatus that's attached to a computer that measures you're lung capacity.
Then the dreaded six minute walk. You walk as far and as fast as you can in a six minute time period. When I initially began these six minute walks I would walk in the hallways in the pulmonary department. It was a rectangular group of hallways, often times people would be coming out of or going into their offices and they had to step aside for you to pass by and during the several years of doing

this, I have to admit it was pretty easy, I don't even think I needed oxygen. Toward the end of my five years of appointments, they changed the route and you walked up and down just one hallway. By this time I was on oxygen. The walk forced you to go around these small orange cones at each end of the hallway and then back again for the entire six minutes. It was also a hell of a lot harder to do those six minutes. You're constantly making those 180 degree turns around these little cones with a lung technician following close behind wheeling a canister of oxygen which is attached to the cannula in your nose (the technicians also must take the six minute walk, probably many times a day, depending on how busy the pulmonary department is). With a lung disease this is murder. By two minutes the oxygen that the nurse pushes alongside you is cranked up to 4 liters as your body is quickly desaturating of oxygen. By 3 minutes you are "feeling the burn". Not in your legs, but in your entire body, by 4 minutes you are exhausted, you're up to 5 liters of O2 and you can barely find the strength or energy to walk, and you feel like you are getting NO oxygen when you breath. I always pushed like hell to walk and not stop, because I wanted to prove to the doctors that I was not ready to have the transplant. Almost always I did well with the walk but toward the end, the real end, I walked on sheer adrenalin alone.

11 am – 1 pm Meet with the nurse, the pre- transplant coordinator, usually Mike Cwalina then the pre-transplant doctor, usually Dr. Marie Budev or Dr. Thomas Olbrych, both brilliant pre and post-transplant care physicians. These doctors KNOW lung and heart transplantation, although they don't perform transplantation surgery they work closely with the doctors that do to facilitate a positive outcome. They do however perform, assist and direct when many vital procedures are implemented or when additional care is needed; including rejection, broncosopies, excess fluid drainage and many other major

health issues such as prescribing medications and ordering additional tests. Their daily professional life is full of vital responsibilities. They are detailed, organized and concerned about your transplant health. They dot every "i", cross every " t" and order a dozen tests prior to the surgery to ensure a positive result.

Sometimes I met with the transplant surgeon, the ENT doctor or the orthopedic doctor for bone density or the cardiothoracic doctor. There was almost always a variation in the sequence of physicians visit to visit but I always met with a pre-transplant specialist.

The major concern of having such as big surgery is surviving it and not having other major health issues which could affect a positive outcome. Every aspect of your body is tested and evaluated. Heart, lungs, liver, kidneys, pancreas, mental health, colon, nose, eyes name it, it was evaluated. And for many tests, it was more than once.

Along the way they discovered I have cirrhosis of the liver. It is not from drinking however. It is from CF, another unfortunate aspect of this deadly disease. The doctors were concerned as to how this would affect my transplant, they found it from a CAT scan, an eventual biopsy didn't even reveal this health issue. My doctors in Cleveland felt it was a problem that could maintain itself for years, maybe forever, or it could stop working within months, in which case a liver transplant was in order. G-d no, I had not even had my lung transplant and I was given the prospect of a liver transplant.

I distinctly remember leaving most appointments full of anxiety, relieved it was over, exhausted and worried.

My Supporting Family

My sisters Candy and Holly always call and ask how I am doing. I get a call from either of them probably 3-4 times a week. No matter how bad I feel on that particular day I always said "Fine". I understand as a sibling myself how difficult it is to hear "Fine", knowing that is an answer of convenience and not reality. I know they would like to hear "fine" and believe I'm fine, but they do not.

The anxiety and stress I put my sisters through is something I am not proud of. I know their lives are already full of daily issues and concerns and they do not need my problems too. Still, the calls are given not out of necessity but out of love and caring. For that I say "Thank you and I love you". I have always had my sisters to rely on and lately my reliance has been greater than ever. The love given to me is something that I can never repay. Thankfully they do not expect anything in return except my gratitude and love.

I talk to my mother daily. This routine started when I finally moved out of her home and into my own. I started calling her in the morning, every day without fail and still do it to this day. The only times I have not is when I was out of town or in the hospital. I have called her almost every morning for almost 30 years.

I can't begin to expound the emotional stress my illness has had on my mother. It's almost as if she is living it too. I know this illness has been just as hard on her as it has been on me. She remains strong on the outside, but knowing her like I do, is crying on the inside.

She often makes me and my family dinners or desserts in an attempt to ease the stress of our day and ease the burden of preparing our evening meals. She will come over in the morning or afternoon and get my daughter on or off the school bus. She drives me around like a chauffer without a complaint. She has always been there for me and I am always able to rely on her love and support. She has given me encouragement and support when I needed it most and pushed me along when I need a shove. My mother has truly been a positive driving force in my life and she knows I love her more than words on this page could say.

My entire family, including my in-laws have been through a lot with me and although I do not usually vocally express myself on the state of my illness (I am not terribly vocal in general), they have a good idea of what I am going through. They know it's not a fun, everyone should do this at least once in your lifetime type of experience, and I'm sure they must feel helpless in their ability to make me feel better. The unconditional love of my family also includes the pain, the sadness, the hopelessness but always the belief that my life will improve in the near future. I am lucky I have them.

My father who lives in Florida also calls me often. It is much harder for him as he has not seen me in a few years because of his own health issues, and is not able to fully confront my troubles like my sisters and mother. I know he feels helpless and wishes there was more he could do, but I understand and know he does what he is able. I am always appreciative of his calls, even if I am not in the mood to talk.

I have been at Women and Children's Hospital for weeks at a time during my "tune up" routines and have seen children that had been admitted before I arrived and were still there when I left who had no visitors. That's NO visitors. How can families, *how can parents* do this to their children. These children have a tough enough time in life with the disease they live with. They are already missing out on just living the life of a child but add into that mix not having the love of your family or parents present and it just makes this child's life that much more difficult. This I could never understand and have never had to worry about. My family visits me whenever they were able, and they visit often. My family understands the difficulty of living for weeks at a time in a hospital room, and they always try to make my stay as tolerable as possible.

As a father I want to comfort these often lonely, wishing to play, wishing to be loved children, but I cannot. When I'm in the hospital I am too sick, plus it's an unwritten rule that you should not be in close contact with another CF patient because germs spread all too easily between us. I think it's something like a three foot rule, which isn't too bad, and when I am in, it seems most people do stick to it.

Me with my mom and my sisters, Candace and Hollis in 2011.

Day to Day Survival   July, 2009

Late in my transplant process, just a few months before my transplant, I think it was the second last time we went to Cleveland for evaluation I had to change the pants I was wearing in the car on the thruway to Cleveland. There was only a rest stop on the New York State Thruway and I decided to change in the back seat of our car, I was no longer driving to Cleveland at this point, my wife was doing that and she pulled over and got out of the car to wait for me to change. I had packed spare clothes as we were staying overnight in Cleveland for a next day appointment. I took off my oxygen and left it in the front seat, got in the back and proceeded to change. Leaving the oxygen in the front seat was a huge mistake. The effort of changing was too much for me. I thought I was going to pass out. I was gasping for air and when I was finished changing and had gotten back into the front passenger seat I immediately put my cannula back on. Although I was breathing in pure oxygen I was still totally depleted of air. I remember being frantic. I simply was not getting enough oxygen into my system. I had cranked up the O2 level higher than usual, in the 6-7 liter range but my lungs were too destroyed to take it in any faster. It was one of the few times I felt helpless and it scared me half to death, which I probably was halfway there anyway. It's been eight years since I first went for a tune-up in WCHOB and those years have taken a huge toll on my body. My health has deteriorated greatly and my body is a shell of what it once was.

My father has come up from Florida shortly after I got home from my Cleveland visit. It is great to see him again. Because of his health he also wears oxygen now; he has COPD. He drove up with his wife and daughter. His wife, he admits, does most of the driving.

Unfortunately I have not been feeling well at all and

have really been struggling with my breathing these past few weeks. With my father in town I am out of the house more than I am comfortable with. Being without oxygen is a tough situation. That means no supplemental oxygen for long periods of time. The daily stress is really too much on me and while I was privately talking with my dad I just broke down. I cried. I cried from the stress, I cried from the struggle, I cried because he was actually here to support and comfort me. I cried because I needed to. This disease is brutal as hell and sometimes you need to let it out. With his familiar arm around my shoulder, I could not hold back the strain of this battle any longer. This year has been hell, and I think back to the day my CF doctor in Buffalo told me it would be.

My father and I at his home in Florida in 2010.

Almost Completely Reliant on Others
September, 2009

I made a call to Jenny Cohen recently to make an odd request. Jenny's the woman that cuts my hair. I had to ask her if she would come to my house so I could get a haircut instead of me going to her. I can no longer get to the salon where she works to have it cut. Again the stress of getting there is more than my body can take. The last dozen or so times I have gone to Jenny I have dreaded it. Not her of course, not getting my hair cut, but the amount of effort it takes to get there. It is exhausting to get my haircut. Crazy!

I am fortunate in that she is an understanding and caring person. I have known her since 5th grade, and have been getting my haircut from her since I was about 35 years old. She knows me, and she knows if I could get to the hair salon where she works I would do it. I think she was a bit surprised to find me standing in my kitchen with a cannula in my nose but hey, I've got to do what I've got to do and this is it. I am reliant on many things now including my family, my wife, oxygen, my vest, my nutritional feeds, and now Jenny. I sit down in the middle of my kitchen on a folding chair and she does her thing. It's not the best of circumstances for her or me but I'm sure she has cut and styled hair many times in similar situations. Things like getting my hair cut at home are probably small inconveniences to Jenny but a huge relief to me, and getting my haircut makes me feel better, at least a little neater and that is a good thing.

My Last Hospital Stay at WCHOB
October, 2009

I have an unscheduled appointment this morning with the doctors at the CF Clinic at Women and Children's Hospital of Buffalo. My usual routine is to sign in on the first floor, go up to the pulmonary lab on the 3rd floor and do my PFT's (Pulmonary Function Tests), get the printed results and go back to the first floor for weight, blood pressure and physical exam. This is when my CF doctor looks over my PFT results, re-checks my blood pressure and weight and discusses my overall health. Sometimes they want blood work which is done at a lab directly adjacent to the lung clinic. They also always want a sputum sample, which I dislike giving. The idea is to cough up a bit of what is festering in your lungs. Any CF patient can get a sputum sample with little effort. You cough it into a small plastic sample cup. The same ones you use for urine samples. Almost always what you cough up is thick and green. Yes, green. This is what is living in your lungs on a normal basis. This is what is slowly killing your lungs. This is what they need to put under a microscope and examine and determine what germs are happily colonizing in your lungs. The two powerful destroyers of your lungs are the germs pseudomonas (sue-doe-moe-nus) and aspergillus (like it sounds). This is what is slowly killing you. I never look at the results of my PFT's anymore. I used to, but it's too depressing to see how much worse you have gotten since the last visit.

These appointments are always anxiety ridden. I know the personnel at the pulmonary clinic try their best to make it as easy and stress-free as possible, but it is still a performance test and most of us fail it miserably. After numerous failures you become "gun shy" to the whole damn thing. It is an inevitable routine that's become a necessary evil. I know however that many CF'ers will cancel an appointment just to NOT have to go through it. I did it, I think once. I knew however that they were more vital to keep than to skip.

Today however is a visit that was not on my appointment calendar. I am too sick to wait for that, I need help today. My mother is driving me to the hospital, I really cannot drive there alone anymore, I've found that breathing is a necessary element in self-reliance, and I no longer have that. Getting showered and dressed in the morning is a struggle of huge proportion and by the time 9 am rolls around and my mom has come I am exhausted and it isn't getting any better.

I wear oxygen all the time now, cough every 30 seconds or so, imagine coughing every 30 seconds or less throughout your waking hours, and I don't mean cough, cough, I mean COUGH, COUGH, COUGH. It's a thick, deep disgusting cough that consumes your body and leaves it weak, rattled and beat. I constantly have to stop wherever I am and try, try so hard to catch my breath, I slump over the kitchen countertop, or kneel on the floor next to the bed, put my arms on the top of the bed mattress and just suck in, hoping to fill my lungs with air and it never happens, there's only more sucking and more hoping. Often times I would lean against my high boy dresser with my arms on top, or if I was taking a shower, I would reach up with my arms raised over my head and lean against the wall of the shower. I found this was relieving to me, having my arms slightly higher, maybe head high. It took the pressure off my swollen, damaged lungs and allowed me to breathe easier. I did this often, most times without even realizing I was doing it and I would just remain there as it was more comfortable, and I needed any comfort I could get. This time I'll feel better, this time I'll feel better, this time will be it, this time I'll catch my breath, this time I'll feel better. Imagine doing this ALL day long. This is how I live.

Today, I struggle to make it into the kitchen and have to stop and lean onto the countertop to catch my breath, I have the portable oxygen with me now, it's cranked up to 5 liters, I need it that high whenever I am moving, or I am in big trouble, it's hard, you have no idea, I pray to G-d you will never feel this way. I am always leery about my portable O2. I'm afraid it will run out before I get to a reliable source of O2, although it's supposed to last 3 hours or so. I know I have to make it out to my mom's car in the driveway, it's tough to walk that distance, probably 30 feet or so, I have to walk down 2 stairs, carry my portable O2, not heavy, but just dragging around my 155lbs. on my nearly six foot frame is a struggle, go through the garage and get into my mom's car, oh g-d, I don't look forward to this, and wish I could just sit in my La-Z-Boy for the rest of the day.

I am ready now, and although I really don't feel any better, I don't feel any worse and that is the sign that I must move now or I won't move at all. And I do, I try to never make it look as bad as it is, I don't want anyone to know the difficulty I am going through. I think to myself, I wish I could always be asleep because that is the only time I am not aware of this desperation.

I get into my mom's car, it doesn't take long, I try to make it look as normal as possible. Once I sit down, I don't move, just concentrate on breathing, sucking in compressed 99% pure air. Just don't move and breath, breath damn it, breath damn it, I feel my heart pumping, I can literally hear it, and hope it doesn't stop, if it does I certainly will know, the pounding feeling and sound are loud enough now. After about 3 minutes I am back to full alert mode and out of all-out crisis mode. I know that will begin again as soon as I move around a bit, such as lifting myself out of this damn car, I dread that. My mom's 86 years young but really an excellent driver and I'm thankful for that, more stress is not what I'm looking for at this point. We get to the hospital, an approximately half hour drive into the City of Buffalo and she drops me off at the curb just in front of the door. OK, I can do this, I have to walk up about 9 steps, they will feel like 100, go thru a vestibule, make a right turn and go down a short hall to the check-in area. Going up those steps is the feeling of going up those 100 steps, except you never took in that last big breath before you did it and now you're breathing through a swizzle stick. Actually though, I'm breathing as hard as I can and 5 liters of O2 is pumping into my lungs through a cannula in my nose.

I make it to the vestibule, a small area about the size of a walk-in closet and have to sit down on a wall heater. At this point I can go no further. My body is spent. It's odd feeling exhausted when you know you have done little actual exertion. People pass in and out, its cold outside but not bad, it's October. Some look at me sitting there on the heater with the cannula in my nose, some rush in or out and don't even notice me. A few children stare as they pass with their mother, (it is a children's hospital). A doctor stops and asks if I need help, I smile, say no thank you and he keeps going. Ten minutes pass, I have been trying to get up and make that right to go down the hallway but really I can't get enough air in my deprived body to do it. Another few minutes pass and FINALLY, finally I get up and go for it. I exit the vestibule, make the right turn, walk two steps and know I cannot go any further. I see the nutritionist, Chris down the hall. I will normally see her during an office visit, and yell to her "Chris", she turns around, she knows my health status. She asks if I need a wheelchair and I can only say "Yes". Soon she comes with one and I sit down, relieved that now someone else is going to do the work for me and I won't have to walk. I was barely able to stand the short time I waited for her, it sounds surreal I know but it's not only true, it's probably not even completely explaining this dire health situation I've found myself in.

Meanwhile, my mom circles the hospital in her car, her cell phone is ready, she is waiting for the call that I will be admitted into the hospital. She will not be surprised, she will be relieved. So will I.

I don't go for PFT's today, I go directly onto the 10th floor of Women and Children's Hospital. The 10th floor houses all the CF patients who are young adults and adults who are here for weeks on end, some stay months, it's tragic. It may seem odd to have adults in a children's hospital, but the disease is a disease you are born with, and most babies, toddlers and children spend part of their youth at this hospital and then their pre-teen, teen, young adult and finally adult time here, G-d willing.

My nurse today, a great guy named Dale takes my oxygen level. He places a pulse-oxy clip-like device on my finger and it reads the oxygen level in my blood stream. It reads low, in the 70's. "You are hypoxic", he says. "Don't move, I'll test you again in a little while".

Hypoxic, big deal, I could have told you that, I think to myself. What I want is for you to make me non-hypoxic. He comes back after 10 minutes and checks my O2 level once more. It's in the 80's, which is better but still not good. I have not moved a muscle since I sat in this hospital room. It's too exhausting. My hospital routine has once again begun. The PIC line is inserted around 12 pm and my first meds. are begun that evening around 4 pm.

The 10th floor of WCHOB has many hospital suites for its' CF patients. They are nicer than most hospital rooms in that they are all singles, they are larger and really made for the long haul, two weeks or more in one room. They all have showers in the bathroom, and a small dining like table. There's sometimes a couch in the room, if not then a few more chairs than an ordinary room. These rooms are unique, just like the people that occupy them. They are designed for a person that is not necessarily bed bound, but still unable to leave a hospital. It took many years for WCHOB to get these suites, they started out with just one and now they have 5.

My doctor eventually comes in and we discuss my deteriorating health although we don't use those terms. It's a conversation of my future really, and that conversation is about lung transplantation and how the dedicated nurses are going to attempt to get me well enough to make it to that transplant. I have had this conversation many times before with various doctors.

I spent the next three weeks getting intravenous antibiotics with little positive results. At some point I was wheeled down to the lung clinic for my usual PFT's. My FEV1 is now at 16% and my FVC at 46%.
I am at a point of no return. Transplantation is soon.
At some point during my stay; the days blend together in a hospital room, my niece Devin comes to visit me. She is 22 years old and I will always remember the day she was born. Today though it was an effort to talk, I know I didn't say much and I didn't even try to hide the fact I was on constant oxygen. She started to cry. Although that took me a bit off guard I couldn't blame her, I was a pathetic sight and I knew it. My wife and family visit me of course, I know they feel helpless in this situation, and always try to keep conversion on light topics and my daughter, whom always makes me feel better.

Rabbi Tanenbaum from Temple Beth Am in Amherst called me today. Temple Beth Am is the temple I belong to. Honestly I have been there only a handful of times since we joined. It has been too difficult to walk and breathe without oxygen to attend services and I won't attend with oxygen. The last service I went to was a memorial service for Susan Wehrle. She was our Cantor and tragically died in the plane crash of Flight 3407, on its' approach to Buffalo/Niagara International Airport on February 12, 2009.

Rabbi Tanenbaum was very nice and his inquiry into my health, my disease and imminent transplant was sincere. I imagine making such a call to a member of your temple that you don't even know and discussing a disease you don't know about is difficult at best. Although I was not very talkative and wasn't up to discussing the complexity of my situation I was happy he made the time in his busy day to extend his support and prayers for me.

At the present time I do not have an appointment at Cleveland Clinic until the beginning of November. I don't believe my Buffalo CF doctor and the Physician's Assistant at Children's felt I was going to make it a whole month and that I needed to be transplant listed immediately. There is talk of transporting me to Cleveland Clinic from WCHOB for an indefinite period of waiting in Cleveland for my transplant. This would mean transporting me directly from one hospital to the other. However I have not gone to committee at Cleveland Clinic for transplantation yet. Going to committee involves your pre-transplant doctor proposing you for transplant listing. The committee is composed of doctors, assistants, surgeons, anesthesiologists and various other health care professionals who meet once a week and go over the health records of those being proposed for transplant. They eventually approve or reject the request for transplantation based on many factors. If you are approved it then goes to the Ohio Dept. of Health for approval which is basically a rubber stamp process.

At some point a call was made from the Physician's Assistant at WCHOB, (thank you Lynn), to the Cleveland Clinic pre-transplant team to impress upon them my need to be listed. You must understand, I was in no rush to hurry the process of transplant along and although I was scared to be transplanted I was still more scared of getting too sick to even be listed at all. The Cleveland doctors try very hard to wait until the last possible day to list you and even through my last Buffalo hospital visit they were reluctant to list me without seeing me first. My neighbor Rob Lederman, who knew of my hospitalization was also instrumental in getting a large benefactor to Cleveland Clinic; Mr. Bob Rich to put a bug into some higher ranking administrators ear to keep the process of getting me listed on track, and during my last week of hospitalization I received a call from a pre-transplant coordinator at Cleveland Clinic.

I remember she called me in my hospital room in WCHOB and told me I was officially listed and to be ready as I could be called in just a few days. I was sitting in a chair next to the door in my hospital room, it was the chair I sat in almost constantly, and slept in also, as I was constantly coughing and could not comfortably lie in a bed, even propped up in bed was difficult and the chair was nearer the sink and the bathroom which although was only maybe 8-9 feet away was still far for me at that point. I was stunned, "a few days, really how can that be, wait; let's talk about this, what do you mean a few days! I haven't been home in almost 3 weeks and I can potentially go directly to Cleveland for who knows how long".

I wanted to see my daughter, my family. I wanted to see her dressed up in her Halloween costume and at least spend a few days at home. I had not seen my daughter much at all in three weeks, maybe twice.

To be honest, I was afraid I was going to possibly die and I really wanted to be with my family just a little more. Look, I know what you're thinking, possibly die, really, isn't that's a bit dramatic. But step into my shoes for a minute. I'm getting a double lung transplant! My existing lungs, as shot as they are, were still MY lungs. They complimented my body and my DNA. Surgeons are planning on taking them both out. After a few biopsies they are throwing them in the garbage! Then they are putting two lungs into that empty chest cavity that were breathing in another human beings body not 6 hours ago! Bless that poor soul who lost their life. These will become my new and improved lungs. They will from that time forward keep me alive! It is a once in a lifetime, put it all on the table (literally and figuratively) opportunity. Hopefully you understand my point of view on this. And thankfully she understood. They put me on the "hold" list. I would not lose my spot on the active listing, but could re-activate myself when I was ready.

I went home after four weeks in WCHOB and spent the end of October and into mid-November believing I would rebound to better overall health, but I was now constantly on oxygen and couldn't walk from the family room to the bedroom without gasping for breath. My days were spent in our second bedroom with 24/7 oxygen and night times with a BiPAP on my face. It was a full face BiPAP covering both my nose and mouth and although uncomfortable it was necessary as it aided my lungs at night when they were most susceptible to losing their ability to function as best as they could.

I existed like this throughout the end of October and into November, barely seeing my daughter in her Halloween costume. Mostly only as she passed by the doorway of the room I was stuck in; visiting a few times and once on Halloween with her costume on, but only for a minute or two. I couldn't blame her. She was excited about Halloween, and I was not exciting. My sister in-law handed out candy at our door that Halloween night, I could hear the trick or treaters, but never saw one child in their costumes. I could not handle such an exhausting task as standing and handing out candy (thank you Dana for that and many other sacrifices you made for the love of your family and your niece).

I literally struggled at taking a shower at this point. I almost never took one anymore and usually just washed my hair leaning over into the shower. That was far easier for me, although still difficult. Honestly the work involved for me to take a shower was unbelievable. I was literally exhausted when I was done and it took about an hour to take it. It was so exhausting that sometimes I didn't even take off my socks before I went in. I figured that could wait until I was out and had regained a bit of strength from the sheer exertion of getting my clothes off and into the damn thing. I must admit, it was a good feeling to take one though and I missed the days when I was able to take a shower without this incredibly ridiculous effort.

So my days and nights went by in this bedroom, my world now. Leaving it was a difficult, arduous task which I made only infrequently. The apprehension of moving out of that chair is burned into my memory and I still cannot believe how much I dreaded it.

Beginning of November 2009   The Final Push

I'm running hard, really hard, my legs are pumping, heart pounding, lungs sucking air, yet it's effortless and I'm celebrating the sheer exhilaration of it. I don't really know what I'm chasing or what's chasing me, I just know I've got to run. So I do. I'm barely breathing heavy and I think I could do this forever.

Then I wake up and reality forces itself on me. The dream I had was a reoccurring one and always ends the same way. I have a BiPAP mask on. The BiPAP mask I'm wearing goes over my head and face, it always reminds me of a fighter jet pilot putting on his oxygen mask before he takes off, but this contraption pushes oxygen into my lungs so my airways open up a bit more and absorb a bit more oxygen and retain less carbon dioxide. When you sleep your oxygen levels go down, so I'm probably in the mid 80's if I'm lucky, on a scale of 100. The BiPAP is new for me and I've only worn it for about two weeks. "Bi-Level Positive Airway Pressure (BiPAP) machines are non-invasive machines that provide positive pressure while a person breathes in and lowers the air pressure when a person breathes out. Thus, the BiPAP has preset pressures: EPAP (exhalation pressure) and IPAP (inhalation pressure). If the sleeping person doesn't take a breath, the BiPAP machine increases pressure, forcing the sleeping person to take a breath. The air pressure then decreases, allowing the person to work less against the airflow pressure to exhale. Because the sleeper's breathing varies, so does the BiPAP's pressure, allowing the pressure drop to vary according to the needs of the sleeping individual. This ability to vary air pressure allows the sleeper to exert less energy to exhale and sleep deeper."[7] Some people however, just can't get used to it, it can be uncomfortable, the tightness on your head can give you a headache if it's not adjusted right and it forms a suction around your face.

There is an oxygen tube attached to the BiPAP mask, the tube runs from the mask through our second room where I basically live and sleep in a La-Z-Boy chair, down the hall and into our master bedroom into a big liquid oxygen canister that supplies me with pure oxygen. The canister is big and probably weights 200 lbs. when full, it rolls on wheels, lasts me about 2 weeks and then a service technician picks it up when it's empty and brings me a new one. It's a new tank every two weeks for about four and a half years.

Another tube attaches to a "button" on my stomach. The button, about the size of a dime has a rubber open-close flap. Sitting behind the button and right next to my skin is a soft plastic spacer, about an inch long, by 1/8 inch deep. It prevents my button from entering into my stomach through the hole that's mid-way up my chest, and just slightly off center. A hard foam stopper in my stomach is attached to a short tube that's attached to the button. It's a "gateway" into my stomach that's not through my mouth. The tube attached to the button feeds me high calorie nutritional liquid, 500 calories per 250ml can at a rate of 180ml per hour. So as I'm sleeping a machine that's attached to an IV pole next to me pumps 2000 calories directly into my stomach each night. I lie in a chair while I'm getting these feeds, and fall asleep to the sound of the pump attached to the IV pole. I've been doing this two and a half years.

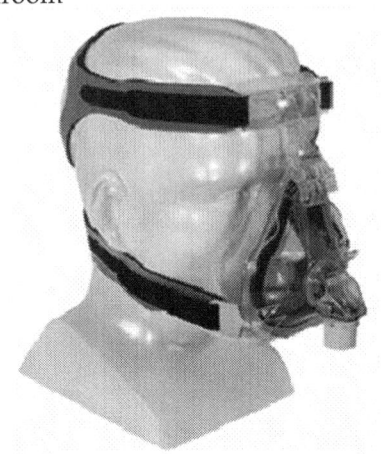

A typical BiPAP mask

It's an odd feeling to say the least. But I'm living an odd life, or what's left of it. This is my reality, not the running, or the effortless breathing or the exhilaration. I have an appointment in Cleveland in mid-November and I'm activating my status on the transplant list. I can live like this no more.

On the "Active List"   November 13, 2009

When Deb and I were traveling to Cleveland for our appointment we discussed my options and I told her I was as ready as I will ever be, life sucked at that point, and honestly, and although I don't feel this way today, I wouldn't have minded dying. I did however mind leaving the people I loved and was very concerned about their well-being, it is not easy being a single parent and I worried Deb could end up as one.

Although I was not "officially on the active list" on the trip to Cleveland, I explained to my wife I was going to ask to be activated at my appointment the next day. She insisted I wait not a minute more and make a call to the pre-transplant coordinator in Cleveland for immediate activation. I made the call and got voicemail, but I made the call, and that seemed to satisfy my wife.

Needless to say, I was bad, and at my November 13th Cleveland appointment, I asked to be officially activated by Dr. Budev. My FEV1 after today's PFT's is 14% and my FVC is 41%. I was told by my doctors in Cleveland that they did not think my wait would be long, mostly because of my body size and of course my poor health condition. At that appointment I distinctly remember Dr. Budev saying to me "I promise you will be fine and you will come out of this OK". Those words made me feel much more at ease concerning this difficult surgery. I even remember saying to my wife on the drive home, "Dr. Budev promised me I would have a successful surgery and be OK, she wouldn't say that unless she was sure".

As soon as you're listed it's a waiting game, with no time-outs. Just because the working day is over and the doctors have gone home, it doesn't mean you can wait until the next day to get a call that lungs are available. The call can come at any time, it's 24/7 from then on.

A few days after my appointment in Cleveland the

phone rang and the answering machine picked up. My wife was at school for parent conferences, and my daughter was at ballet class. After the answering machine ended its' usual "please leave a message" request, I heard a male voice on the machine and I instantly knew this was no ordinary message.

I got "the call" on November 18th, four days after I was officially listed.

I picked up the phone and I'll never forget the man on the other line telling me almost immediately.
"Hello, This is Mark from the Cleveland Clinic transplant program. Am I speaking with William Mahaney"? "Yes, it is". I managed to spit out. "Congratulations, William, we have lungs for you, we're almost sure they're good, the match is right and we need you to come to Cleveland as soon as possible". I know I was fumbling with my words, with my thoughts, it was a shock to hear, and to know my life was officially in the hands of another and I could not prevent the outcome at this point. Your instinct is to say no, but your intellect says yes, yes it's time. Don't disappoint others and don't disappoint yourself by saying no I can't, or no I don't want to. This opportunity will only come around once, these may be the perfect lungs, they may not be the perfect lungs. It is a chance you must take. I remember the man on the line saying, "don't be nervous, you'll be fine, this is a great chance and a huge life giving opportunity". He gave me all the specifics, where to go when we got to the hospital, who to ask for, etc. and honestly I don't remember a thing he said. Again, thank g-d for Deb, as she was able to keep it together and get the proper instructions. He had called her on her cell phone just prior to me and she had her wits about her to correctly get all the vital information.

Once I hung up with him, Deb immediately called and told me what I already knew. I was still in a state of shock however. I was scheduled for a midnight surgery. I had *never* had any surgery in my 52 years and now I was about to have a huge surgery! Deb got home almost immediately and after getting a few things together; we had already packed her clothes and mine in preparation, we waited for my daughter to get home from ballet. After saying my good-byes and telling my daughter how much I loved and will miss her, Deb and I headed for Cleveland.

Potentially not having much time sure makes a person think about the time he has. The drive is 3 hours, it was a nervous, anxious drive and Deb and I talked about many things, we covered all outcomes although I remember Deb really keeping a positive outlook and ignored the negatives as she believed they were not necessary to bring up. That kind of positive outlook really put me more at ease, and again I thank her for that.

It was a rainy night entering the greater Cleveland area and I felt a real feeling of foreboding. I also felt a feeling that my oxygen could run out and that would piss me off more than the foreboding part.

Pulling into the huge semicircle drop-off/pick-up area of the new Cleveland Clinic Sydell & Arnold Miller Family Pavilion was a bit surreal. It was always packed with cars and people and wheelchairs and shuttle buses. Tonight it was very quiet. As we pulled up to the curb a man in a red sports jacket was ready and eager to assist us. These men and women are all around the hospital, answering questions, assisting in getting wheelchairs, opening car doors and even walking with you to a scheduled appointment or unfamiliar area of the hospital. They make the anxiety and confusion of being there more manageable.

I needed a wheelchair, which he got immediately and he wheeled me into the new large atrium of the new heart and vascular complex. It is a big open space, high ceilings, probably 40 ft., with new, modern furniture. It was exceptionally quiet that evening. The time was now about 10 pm. Everyone had gone home except for some miscellaneous stragglers and employees who probably were working their usual round of night shift.

Deb went and parked the car. She was back almost immediately and the red suited man directed us to the proper elevator to take us up to the ICU.

For me the elevator ride up was almost like going to the firing squad, and although I can smile about it today, that's how it felt then. We first entered into a large waiting room. It was beautiful and still new, a bit cold and impersonal but I guess that's what an area of this nature is best suited for and I was wheeled directly through the room past a security desk and through two doors and into the ICU.

I would watch this complex being built from the Crile Building and at each appointment. I would see the progress made on this structure and wonder what it was going to look like and contain when it was completed. Well, today I knew the answer to that question. It was going to contain me!

The Cleveland Clinic Sydell & Arnold Miller Family Pavilion is huge and the transplant surgery and ICU is a brand new state-of-the-art complex that is similar to a small city of activity and action.

Entering the ICU, I remember it was oddly quiet though, it almost seemed empty (which it never was), and I was directed to a bed at the end of the unit. I was given the usual blood pressure, heart rate, pulse ox. all the routine procedures and asked to take off my clothes, put on a gown, oh those hospital gowns, and wait.

I remember my sister and mom coming in after about ½ hour. When they first heard the news that lungs were available for me they too picked up their already packed suitcases and probably flew out the door. My poor mom and my family, such stress I put them through!

I don't think much was said, we were all uneasy. I then met the doctor who was to perform the operation. Dr. David Mason, a brilliant, humble and caring man who exuded the confidence necessary to calm an anxious patient and his family. He explained the surgical procedure in non-medical terminology so we were able to grasp its' complexity. He then informed us that he was just waiting for the final inspection on the lungs to be sure they were good to go, and if they were good I would be cleared for and prepped for surgery.

   It was a tense wait, and I think it was less than one hour. At some point the anesthesiologist came to meet me, introduced himself, again explained the basic procedure of the operation, how the incision was going to be made, the steps to take out my old lungs and put in the new ones, the approximate time of the surgery, assuming they don't run into any complications then asked me if I had any questions. "Yes, I said, is there an easier way"? "If there were, we would have it." was his reply.

My New Lungs   November 19th, 2009

I was informed at 11 pm the donor lungs were healthy and the procedure was a go. Then things went fast. The anesthesiologist came back for me just a few minutes later. As he was wheeling me in my bed out of the ICU and to the operating room he said to me "Let's go get you a new pair of lungs." It sounded like a good idea to me. I was taken into surgery at 11:30 pm. I honestly don't remember some very important things just prior to heading into the OR, things which I am ashamed to admit. I don't really remember saying good-bye to my daughter in Buffalo, she was taken out of her ballet class back in Buffalo to say good-bye to me, I remember being with her, but I don't remember what was said, nor anything that I said to any of my family, my mom or sister or even my wife. I remember they were all there, just not the final words spoken. I don't know if the drugs washed that from my memory, anxiety took over or simply that nothing major really was said between us. I find it very hard to believe I did not have any meaningful conversation with my wife or child prior to potentially seeing them for the last time though. That part really bothers me... really bothers me to this day. How could there have been no lasting memory of my final expression of total love I have for my wife and daughter or my family? I was not afraid of dying at this point because I felt so lousy, but I was afraid of leaving my wife and child to fend for themselves. How could I not have told them all the important things I felt? How could I not have expressed all they mean to me. How, how could I not have?

My surgery thankfully was uneventful. It lasted approximately 7 hours. For my double-lung transplant, a large "clamshell" incision was made that exposes the entire front portion of my chest. "A clamshell incision extends from one armpit to the other, under the rib cage, so that the chest opens like a clamshell. The breastbone is cut in two places, removed, the rib case is opened up and the lungs and other vital organs are exposed. For double lung transplants, the surgeon first decides which lung to remove and replace first. The failing lung is collapsed, its blood vessels are tied off, and its main airway (bronchus) is cut. The old lung is removed, and the donor lung is positioned in the chest. The airway is reconnected, and then the lung's blood vessels are reattached. Once the new lung is in place, the surgeon looks inside it with a telescope (bronchoscopy). The doctor will confirm that the lung looks pink and healthy inside and will remove any blood or excess mucus from the airway. Once one lung is transplanted (usually the lung with the poorest function), it is followed by the remaining lung. In about 10 percent to 20 percent of these transplants, the patient is connected temporarily to a heart-lung bypass machine, which pumps blood and supplies it with fresh oxygen."[12] By 7 am the next morning I had two new lungs. I was unknowingly to spend the next week in this space in the ICU, it is slightly separated from the rest of the unit and I believe was reserved for lung transplant patients, another double lung transplant patient was beside me I later found out as I became more aware of my surroundings. I believe the lung transplant patients are given a bit more separation from the rest of the patients because of potential infection to the lungs through the airways. That is just my opinion, not necessarily a fact.

  Six chest tubes had been inserted during surgery, these drained excess fluids and blood out of my chest cavity into bags that had to be emptied frequently along with a Foley catheter to urinate and an IV to receive numerous meds. I remember two chest tubes being pulled after about 5 days in the ICU. I was wheeled straight back into a private area, far behind where my bed was normally positioned and then I was turned at a 45 degree angle. A curtain was closed to shield me from prying eyes. There were doctors all around me and one doctor was examining my chest tubes. He gave me instructions as I lay there on the bed. "I'm going to count to three" he said, "at three I want you to take in a deep breath and hold it until I tell you to let it out". I did as he said, me and the doctors in this private area behind where my bed usually was positioned and with two separate and painful as hell tugs, two more chest tubes were out. This definitely did happen! What did not happen: there was no private area behind my bed, or no turning me at a 45 degree angle. I later figured this out, but only days later when my mind was clearer of the morphine induced medication. My chest tubes were actually pulled right there in my usual spot in the ICU with the privacy curtain closed. Two chest tubes were pulled at some time which I don't remember at all and the last two I had for almost my entire 4 weeks in Cleveland, the last one being pulled on the day I was given the thumbs up to come back home.

What I learned about the ICU: it is NOT quiet as was my first impression. It is a beehive of constant controlled activity, there is no privacy and the nurses, specially trained for the ICU are excellent. Each nurse is assigned only one or two patients and it is their job to constantly care for and monitor them. They are understanding, patient and professional. The women in the bed next to me also received a double lung transplant. The two of us were separated by the usual thin privacy curtain, so it was hard not to be aware of her situation. I know we all have our different issues when going through such a serious operation and hers was she could not seem to come out of the anesthesia. She was in a deep slumber for almost the whole time I was in ICU. Her transplant was within a day of mine +/- but she was in no hurry to wake up. Her nurse would come up to her and almost yell at her. Mrs. Smith, can you hear me, Mrs. Smith, can you hear me, wake up

Mrs. Smith, do you know where you are Mrs. Smith, Mrs. Smith can you hear me. This went on for about a minute or two, almost always with no response. The nurse would leave, a doctor would come, examine her, question the nurse and leave. Then amazingly, one day Mrs. Smith would be alert and talking, then the next day dead asleep, no response. Her husband came in daily, stayed and left looking very disappointed. I don't know what happened to Mrs. Smith, I was transferred up to a private room eventually and she was still in her deep slumber in her bed next to mine at the end of the ICU.

   The lung surgery was a shock to my body and especially my kidneys. They were basically no longer working and I received my first kidney dialysis treatment from a portable dialysis machine in the ICU. The procedure lasted 24 hrs. and was administered through an IV inserted into a vein in my neck. By now I really felt like I had something coming out of literally every part of my body, so when the doctor inserted the catheter into my neck, I felt like OK, now my neck, I can live with that for a while, no big deal. And with tubes going into seemingly every part of your body, you feel like a science experiment. You basically can't move unless someone moves you and many times in the ICU I was literally picked up by 2 men who would grab my bed sheet at the head and foot of the bed that I was lying on and lift me off the bed and into a chair. Shortly after surgery, I don't remember if it was one or two days I asked to be put into a chair which I think surprised my nurse and given instructions to get me up as soon as possible, she was thrilled for me to ask. I did get out of bed that day, and then for days after for one reason or another I was unable to. Eventually I would try each day to get out of bed and when I was ready a team of two men had to be called, I think once or twice it was two women. I tried and usually succeeded in getting out of the chair they carried me to and onto the bed by myself with the help of a nurse. He or she would lift my legs up and into bed. The hard part was not the getting into bed, it was all the tubes and lines that were attached to me that I had to avoid pulling or lying on or kinking, THAT'S what made life difficult.

There was nothing more embarrassing than having a bowel movement in the ICU. You long for a private bathroom. How could I have to poop when I haven't even eaten anything in 4 days? Well, after 4 or 5 days I did and let me tell you it was not a pleasant experience. I would tell my nurse; she would get a bed pan, roll you over on your side, put the bed pan under you and roll you on top of it. Oh my g-d, how embarrassing! She left and shut the privacy curtain for you to do your business. This sucked! It was uncomfortable to lie on a bedpan, it was uncomfortable to shit into a bed pan and it was also uncomfortable to have nothing between you and a stranger but a damn curtain. It was also an unnatural feeling to be lying flat and going to the bathroom. The feeling of going this way was even more challenging simply because your butt was slightly more raised than your head or your feet as the bedpan was maybe three or so inches in height. Your instincts tell you it shouldn't be done. If you were lucky you did your business, called the nurse, she rolled you over on your side, took the bed pan and cleaned your butt with a baby wipe. Again, so embarrassing. Often times it was not that neat and easy and you made a mess of yourself which required multiple baby wipes, or you really filled the bed pan, or you just plain stunk up the place. Did I mention I had not eaten anything, so how the hell did I have so much damn poop! So not fun.

My second last night in ICU, a code blue was sounded, it was an electronic voice, no expression just repeating in a calm, but steady sound - Code Blue, E wing, Code Blue, E wing, Code Blue, E Wing, someone was dying and Deb and I watched in awe as nurses and doctors seemed to come out of nowhere to save this person's life. It seemed as everyone was running, and when it was over and the patient was again stable there were some high fives and handshakes then the nurses and doctors went their own way and all was back to normal. It lasted less than 10 minutes but I remember Deb and I looking at each other with, I think, fear and amazement at the job these dedicated people perform on a daily basis.

I remember Deb coming in today. This is a first. I was sitting in a chair. I continue to make progress. I was given my first solid food. It has been 7 days since I have eaten. It was gelatin, cherry or strawberry, I know it was red, and it was fantastic. Eating was not as difficult as I thought, it was a little hard getting used to swallowing food again though, it seems like those parts of my body did not want to work quite as well as they used to. Eating was another big milestone in my recovery and being able to eat and swallow food was a step in the right direction.

Today is Thanksgiving and I called my mom this morning from Deb's cell phone. She seemed quite surprised to hear my voice. I'm glad I called her. I believe it takes a bit of the anxiety off her to hear me. My first real meal, which was fish, (didn't eat) came on Thanksgiving evening, I had eaten the gelatin during the afternoon. How could they start me out with such a disgusting meal! I sat in my chair and ate just a bit of the other things on my tray, soup, pudding, nothing much but it was a start. My wife had gone to visit her cousins who happened to live in another part of Ohio. She drove to their home, about one hour away for a well-deserved Thanksgiving holiday meal.

Eating solid food, being able to leave my bed, these were all measures of success. And with success brings rewards-

The Waldorf Astoria Floor and Other Happenings

Finally the day came when I was transferred onto a regular floor and it was like having a suite at the Waldorf Astoria compared to the ICU. It was a private room with a huge flat screen TV mounted on the wall, a PRIVATE BATHROOM and real food from a pretty diverse menu. The bed had a remote control attached to it so you could adjust the bed, turn the lights on and off, operate the TV and call the nurses' station. Heaven!

Soon after being put into a private room I noticed something unusual happening to my body. It was getting bigger. It looked like I was getting fatter. I found out from the doctors that I was retaining fluid. Not just fluid, but FLUID! My legs and arms were the first to retain and they got to be big, really big, big like Popeye arms. The fluid would enter into the lower part of my arms when they were left down or hanging. Gravity would fill them and wa-lah; Popeye arms. At one point they were so fluid filled that my skin would begin to tear just a little and this yellowy fluid would run down my arms. It would happen in various places, but once those tiny tears in my skin would occur it was not uncommon to get my gown or a bed sheet, or a pillow wet and they would have to be changed. The same would occur with my legs.

In many ways my legs were more difficult, because the walking aspect of recovery with additional weight became another challenge to work through. My respiratory nurse was a no nonsense woman and she believed walking was essential to getting better. She expected and demanded it. She would ask me as soon as she saw me if I had walked yet that day, and how much I had walked yesterday.

No slippers fit my feet, they looked like big beanbags with fat toes and my legs were near bursting with excess fluid. Often times I could not pull myself off the toilet because of the excess weight on my body. I literally gained 40 extra pounds of water weight in a matter of one week. The fluid eventually settled into my midsection area also and my penis and my testicles looked like tennis balls, also making walking uncomfortable. I could literally feel them rubbing against my fat legs.

When the phlebotomist came in to take my blood work which they did 4 or more times a day, they would look at my arms and hands which were filled with excess fluid and walk away, saying there was no way they could locate a vein. When they did attempt to extract the blood from my veins their syringes would usually get a vial full of fluid, a light yellow color and the syringe would have to be discarded. There was one phlebotomist who was excellent though. He literally pushed the fluid away from under my skin to reveal a good vein, then before the area would fill in again with fluid he would insert the needle into the vein and extract the blood. A master at work!

By the time my stay in Cleveland was over my veins were a wreck. They had been punctured so many times that the phlebotomists actually had a difficult time finding a decent spot to draw blood from. I always had an IV needle and line in one or the other arm, so it made the phlebotomist task that much more arduous!

I can't begin to tell you the effort it was to get up and walk to the bathroom. It wasn't because my lungs were not working, or just because my body was full of excess fluid, although that did not help matters, it was because I was attached to so many damn tubes! I had a catheter for my urine which was attached to a urine bag, approximately the size of a 10" X 8" rectangle when empty. Usually it was at least partially filled and had to be emptied every few hours. The trick with this bag and catheter line was NOT to pull it! It went into a very sensitive part of my anatomy and when it was accidentally pulled, well you can figure out what went with it.

I had two chest tubes, one on each side. The left one was small, about the size of a straw, it was soft and flexible and went into a small clear bag, like a racquet ball size egg that filled with draining fluids from that part of my chest. It was emptied every 3-4 hours, sometimes more and it drained a kind of yellow, pink color fluid. My right chest tube was somewhat larger, and was inserted when I started to retain excess air in my right chest cavity. It replaced a small one like I had on my left side about 1 week into my stay in a regular room. The larger draining tube was inserted in my bed, in my room by a superb young doctor. It was placed between two ribs and into my chest about 3-4 inches, then stitched in so it wouldn't come out with daily movement. This approximately ½" wide tube was a hard plastic material going into my chest and came out about 8 inches. A soft flexible tube attached to it and had a length of about 4 feet leading into a drainage measuring box device. This whole science experiment thing that was going on with me was scary yet amazing all at the same time.

  When I walked, and remember I walked similar to Frankenstein with my fluid filled legs, I would put the box filled with chest fluid on the seat of a wheelchair, then the urine bag would be hung onto the arm of the wheelchair, I would safety pin the small fluid bag on my left to my gown so it didn't just hang out of my chest, (that was uncomfortable), disconnect my heart monitor from the wall outlet and then I would put on a surgeon's mask and head out into the hall to make my rounds. This consisted of walking around the floor, it was a big rectangle of hallway so I could literally do laps. Sounds easy, right… it wasn't. It seemed nothing on me worked well, except and thank g-d, my lungs. It was a real effort to walk those damn halls, Deb made me do it, without her I probably would be still on that floor in that room. She literally forced me to walk, forced me to exercise, forced me to get out of bed or out of a chair. She really was my inspiration, and without her I could not have done it.

She would come in daily and endure my bad moods, my whining, my dissatisfaction, my discomfort ALWAYS with a good attitude and disposition. How she did it I don't know. As much as I was happy for her to go home to Buffalo to see my daughter and spend time with her family, I really missed her when she was gone.

I called my father for the first time since before my transplant. I didn't call him after I received the "it's a go" call from Cleveland. I was too distracted and really totally forgot. I think he was hugely relieved to hear my voice. I was actually coherent enough to carry on a short but happy conversation. Knowing that your son is doing well after a major surgery is great but hearing it directly from your son is much more comforting. The room phone was one of the things about my hospital stay that always annoyed me. The phone which was on the far side of my bed, near the window and simply did not have a long enough cable to reach to the side of the room where the chair and the bathroom and the sink and my heart monitor and my IV pole and I was. This is where I always sat yet the phone was between me and my bed on a nightstand and it was no easy feat to get around that bed. I was simply attached to too much on a constant basis to be able to roam. Eventually Deb bought a 20 foot extension cable for under $10 from Rite Aid. That's when I was finally able to call my dad and actually use the phone.
That major obstacle was fixed with a measly $10 cable. I'm always amazed at the amount of money that's thrown into these high tech specially designed hospital rooms and then the little things that make the room much more livable for the patient are completely forgotten. And of course actually getting a staff member to get you an extension cable for the phone is next to impossible. It's far easier asking for a new bed, (which I did and got) than a phone

cable.

The first week-end in December Deb was gone to watch Mikaela in The Nutcracker. She loves dancing in it, she's good at it and it filled her days after school with an activity that distracted her from Deb being away. As much as she knew where Deb was and that it was only a matter of time before she would again be permanently home it had to be difficult for her. With both parents 300 miles away for essentially eight weeks I'm sure it was not easy. Thank g-d for Nutcracker.

Deb's birthday was that week-end also. She turned 41. A birthday that although I missed I am glad she spent it with her twin sister Dana her family and of course Mikaela.

My sister Holly came during that period and she too was a blessing to have there. Look, it sounds ridiculous, but I couldn't do the simple things, like get to the telephone, get into bed, walk to the sink or bathroom without assistance. She was also a huge help.

The gowns I wore every day for almost thirty days were made of paper thin fabric. It was a light, flimsy patterned material that was tied in the back, so often your butt stuck out. There was nothing to it really, I was cold ALL the time. Remember I had nothing on under this cotton "dress" not even underwear. We eventually figured out to use two gowns, duh, one open in the back, one open in the front. This afforded me a bit of privacy, but believe me, I had long ago left all my dignity at the entrance of the ICU.

My Daily Routine on the Transplant Floor

   Each day I went about the same routine. At around midnight I took my oral meds., at 2:30 am an X-Ray technician came in and took an X-ray while I lay in bed, "Are you Mr. Mahaney, OK Mr. Mahaney, I'm going to be taking an X-ray of your chest, when where you born, good, can you lean forward just a little, good, now I'm going to put this behind your back, lean forward a little more, this will be a little uncomfortable, now don't move, don't move, good OK, we're done, thank you Mr. Mahaney, do you want this door shut, OK goodnight, about 3:30 am my blood was drawn, if they could find their way past the fluid, (at night I would sleep with my arms propped up by two folded pillows, so the fluid would run into my elbow area so the phlebotomist could more easily access my veins for my bloodletting ceremony), at 6 am I took my morning medications. About that time I would be weighed. What a pain in the butt that was. Getting out of bed was amazing difficult. I had to be careful of a urine catheter and urine bag that hung on the side of the bed, a chest tube that lay across my body at night went to the attached box sitting on the floor, my heart rate monitor which was a small but pretty heavy box and attached to me by small round electrode leads all over my upper torso had to be put in the upper left pocket of my gown and the gown that showed all, and I mean all, as I could not yet wear underwear. With the added water weight, it was all quite a sight. At 6:30 am I received my first IV med., at 7:30 am my surgeon visited me to review my progress.

Dr. Mason is a man with a very positive outlook considering all the possible negatives in a operation like the one I had. I did have a few negatives, like for example my kidneys had shut down, and I had a possible tear in one new lung, anyway I'm not complaining, just complications, yet he kept his attitude very upbeat. At 8:30 am my breakfast came, I got to pick what I wanted to eat the day prior. Usually I had eggs, pancakes and juice and milk. It was always a little more challenging eating my breakfast with an IV line in my arm, but it was a tolerable inconvenience.

The whole time I was in the hospital I was thirsty, and nothing and I mean nothing satisfied my thirst. It felt like sometimes certain bottled waters which I normally enjoyed, made me even more thirsty. I can only blame it on the dry air in that hospital, it was like the Sahara in there. Coming and going, I think you did not experience it, but being there 24/7 was brutal. Within a day of leaving the hospital the thirst problem disappeared.

Somewhere in the morning chaos; mornings were always hectic, then the rest of the day dragged on, between breakfast and Deb coming, my respiratory therapist would give me inhaled medications and have me do a spirometry. She would give me the medication, leave and take care of another patient, come back when my first medication was done, switch me over to another inhaled medication, leave and come back in the five or so minutes it took for the medication to be taken, then have me do a spirometry breathing test. At around two weeks after my transplant my respiratory therapist told me I would no longer need any artificial oxygen support. I had been extremely dependent on oxygen and was actually scared to take myself off it. I wasn't emotionally ready to give it up. She disagreed with me, but let me keep it on just at night. That ended quickly however, and after just two more nights she took away my cannula and my oxygen support was gone. What a strange feeling. This is after all what I had hoped to someday live without. But no oxygen support was a scary, strange feeling and it took a few days to get used to.

Deb arrived at about 9-10 am, always the highlight of my day. She was always in a good mood and had more patience than you could imagine. She was a saint, she was also my butler. She got something to drink for me, set up my lunch or dinner tray for me, helped out the nurses with such menial tasks such as emptying my urine bag and helping me to the bathroom. She made sure I brushed my teeth at some point during the day, washed my face and even attempted to wash my hair in the bathroom sink. She made sure I got up and moved around also. She got a wheel chair to steady myself and put my various boxes and bags onto, helped me when I walked solo, making sure I was steady and didn't fall. She was also my lifeline to the outside world, to what was going on besides being poked or stabbed or weighted or examined. She told me about the weather as my window looked onto a courtyard of generators and pipes and walls of another section of the hospital and theirs looked onto mine. She updated me about our daughter, what she was doing, how she was managing with both her parents gone and what was going on in my or her family.

My lunch was always full of Jell-o or pudding or yogurt or ice cream. They served a pretty good and diverse lunch but those were the foods that were easiest and tasted the best to eat. Many times I was in such pain I had a hard time concentrating on food and couldn't eat until I had some pain medication in me. These nurses were busy people and asking for pain medication didn't always mean you got it right away. The wait, probably no more than 15-20 minutes always felt much, much longer. Deb was always there to make sure I ate as much as possible during lunch and would always offer to get me anything I wanted.

During lunch and throughout the morning I was getting an IV of some medication, my nurse was always coming in and switching the bags of medication from one to another to another. Just when I thought I would be free of that damn pole another would be hooked on and I would be stuck to it again. I learned to hate that pole. It really got on my nerves and I would complain to my nurse who was a strict by-the-book, experienced, no-nonsense kind of gal. That pole drove me crazy and complaining did me no good what-so-ever. At times the IV pump was not even delivering medication any longer, and had turned off but I was still hooked up to it just waiting for a nurse to unhook me. I was crazy, crazy, crazy!

Around 3 pm my wife had me go to the bathroom and then we would walk the hallways. She was adamant about making me get up and walking and if I could not come up with a good excuse not to, we walked! She always kept a wheel chair in the shower of my bathroom for me to load my bags and boxes so I could walk more unencumbered.

After walking she made me do leg exercises and arm exercises. I was really having a problem with my right leg and could not move my foot much. The physical therapist would come in three or four times a week, but wasn't exactly sure why it was gimpy, it was eventually believed that the epidural I had received in the ICU damaged a nerve and caused the "foot drop". The "foot drop" lasted into February, about 3 months.

I sat around a lot, watched far too much TV and was exceptionally bored with my circumstances. I tried to get into reading a book or two, but didn't seem to be able to concentrate on them. Don't get me wrong, I was not unhappy with my positive results of the transplant, it was just a long, slow, difficult journey that I was in the process of making to my future good health.

Deb would usually leave for a while, get a snack or do some schoolwork or make some calls or just roam around the shops in the new Sydell & Arnold Miller Family Pavilion. She eventually would wheel me to the new section of the hospital and we would "shop" together.

Dinner came and went, that was around 5-6 pm, you can imagine dinner in a hospital, I don't need to go into any more detail on that. I will say, it wasn't bad, it wasn't good. Deb would usually go and have something to eat, or sometimes bring something back to my room and eat with me, she is a saint, then around 8 pm she would leave.

After that it was all me...and believe me, I wished it wasn't. It's amazing how difficult it is when you have no help. Everything is hard. If the tray table was just out of reach, it was a pain retrieving something from it. It took a good forty five minutes to stand up and set up my bed for the evening then attempt to get into it myself, dragging my boxes and various tubes and lines with me. Little, insignificant things, they were tremendously difficult! I think the nurse's position was to help a patient with maneuvering around and providing assistance when necessary, but that it was up to the patient to become as independent as possible during this time.

I received my last respiratory treatment at around 10 pm. Sometimes in bed, sometimes just before I got in. Then more oral meds. at midnight and the process would begin all over again.

This was my routine with slight variations each day, thankfully Deb kept the often monotonous hospital stay much more tolerable.

Kidney Issues

It soon became apparent that my kidneys were in no hurry to wake up and start working and you know… you really do need them to keep on living, so it was decided I would need additional kidney dialysis. When I could manage to get upright I was put in a wheel chair and taken to the dialysis department, sometimes I had to be taken by hospital gurney and I'm sad to say even the process of getting onto a gurney was a difficult, time-consuming one.

I was taken through a maze of hallways and elevators to finally arrive at the dialysis department. The dialysis department is a huge area with dozens of beds, each with a flat screen TV mounted overhead. In the center of the room is the nurses/technicians station. One wall is a bank of windows that looks out onto the huge round fountain and front entrance of the Sydell & Arnold Miller Family Pavilion.

The technician attached the dialysis machine via the Quinton IV line that had to be replaced in my neck. My first line was placed in the ICU, but they had to move it at some point and make it a more permanent Quinton IV when it was determined I would need additional dialysis. The Quinton was connected and circulated your blood through the dialysis machine, cleaned it of the toxins and excess fluids and replaced it back into your bloodstream. The amount of time this took, I believe depended on how extreme your kidney failure was. My longest time was 4 hours, minus the ICU 24 hour session. Many of the beds were occupied with the same patients when I came in for dialysis as when I left. I went to dialysis only 3 times. Each time after I came back they would say I should feel better and have more energy. I don't think I ever did, but I knew that more energy or not, the dialysis was what was needed to stay healthy and alive.

My First Bronchoscopy

About 10 days into my stay on the hospital floor my X-ray revealed a shadow which indicated trapped air between the lung and chest cavity wall. When you pushed against my skin on my chest, sides or stomach it made a crunching sound, like Rice Krispies in milk, you know, snap, crackle, pop. The doctors felt the excess air was possibly due to a tiny hole in my lung and air was escaping into my chest cavity, not a good thing as it could rather easily result in a collapsed lung.
They would check on this daily, it was not hard to hear the crunchy sound if you just applied a little pressure to my skin. It eventually spread all the way up my neck and it was decided that they should go in and investigate as it didn't seem to be subsiding. I had a bronchoscopy. This is where they put a camera down into your lung usually through your nose and examine it for various things including tears or cuts in the lung from the surgery, infection, rejection, etc. They also will take a biopsy of your lung to examine for rejection or infection. The first part of a bronchoscopy is to numb your gag reflex and they do this by having you inhale a vaporized medication. Then you are put into a twilight sleep through an IV. A bronchoscope is directed through your nose down your airway and into your lung where they are able to view the area and take a tissue sample. By the time you are aware of what's happened, the procedure is over.

Nothing major could be seen and it was believed the leak was very small and would heal itself, however I had to get rid of the excess trapped air in my chest cavity, so it was then they decided a larger chest tube in my right side. The one they put in was a ½ inch rigid plastic as opposed to a ¼ inch soft flexible tubing that I had in my left. The rigid tube was attached to a soft flexible tube about 5 feet long that was attached to a drainage box that measured the fluid and trapped air exiting my chest. The box was about the size of a laptop computer with a handle on it and anywhere I went, it came with me. This rigid tube was really uncomfortable. No it hurt, it hurt a lot, and my primary reason for pain medication was from that tube. It was also the last one taken out of me on the day I left Cleveland and went home to Buffalo.

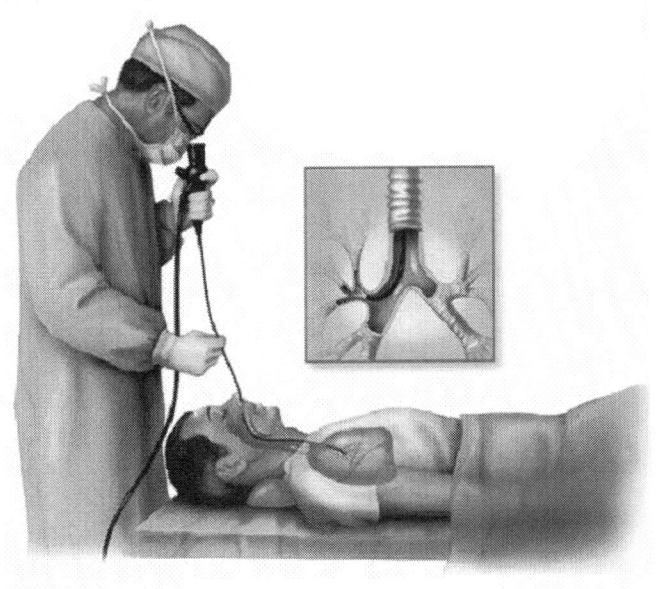

A bronchoscopy procedure

Foley In The Smallest of Holies

Usually a Foley is inserted just prior to surgery in the prep room and then removed in the ICU or when you get into your room on the hospital floor. At some point it was decided to take out my Foley catheter in my hospital recovery room. It was an easy process, just drain the small inflated sack of water in my bladder and pull it out. Now I just had to urinate on my own. But by the end of the day I had not, which was a sign that something was wrong, probably either with my bladder or my prostate. That evening another Foley was reinserted into my poor penis and bladder. It hurt going in, but they got it in and immediately I was peeing into the bag attached to the Foley. My bladder was obviously not empting on its' own. The bag filled in no time. Toward the end of my stay at the hospital, I think it was maybe the last week, it was decided to pull my Foley again. I remember I really wasn't thrilled about them pulling it. The next day the Foley came out first thing in the morning and I was given the day to urinate once again. As hard as I tried I could not urinate and by the end of the day it was again decided to re-insert the Foley catheter. It hurt going in, but after a few pushes it entered into my bladder. For the remainder of the week the Foley stayed in. A day before I was released they wanted to again pull the catheter which made me really anxious. Again nothing. In the evening a very young and probably still a bit inexperienced yet good male nurse tried to re-insert my Foley catheter. It hurt like hell and let me tell you, there is great pain in having someone attempt to shove a small long rubber tube up your penis and past an enlarged prostrate. He could not do it so it was pulled out. My female nurse, the by-the-book nurse gave me a Percocet, or maybe it was two, and gave me a ½ hour and then went about inserting it. Really jamming it past my prostate. I could literally feel it be pushed up to where my enlarged prostrate was, get stuck, shoved into again, then again, and finally past my poor prostrate. It HURT. I remember lying on top of my hospital bed swearing and screaming during the process. I was finally put on Flomax after my last Foley was inserted as my obvious enlarged prostrate was not allowing me to pee on my own. Thank g-d for Flomax, a drug that shrinks the prostate and allows you to have an easy stream of urine. I take it to this day. The next time I had that catheter pulled, which was when I was home from Cleveland, I prayed to pee and thankfully I did.

Done with the Hospital Routine

My every movement was stiff and uncomfortable. My right leg was not working properly, and I could not walk normally. It felt as though I had a stroke on my right side, at least with my right leg. Simply put, I was one wobbly, drunken looking patient who could topple over at any moment, in a flimsy hospital gown with my ass sticking out the back, carrying a box with a tube going into me and a urine bag with a tube obviously also attached to me and wearing a surgical mask. I probably smelled because I wasn't able to take a shower for the entire duration of my stay in Cleveland Clinic. I had not been able to shave with a blade razor because they were concerned about me cutting myself and as I was on blood thinners, my blood would not coagulate normally. Trust me, I was not a GQ cover guy, I looked bad. But I knew I would get better and that is what I had to focus on.

I have now begun to sort my medications by myself. This is the sign they are getting ready to discharge me. Initially in ICU my meds. were all intravenous, now that I am into a regular room I receive almost all of them orally. The nurses give them to me at the scheduled intervals and I take them. Easy peasy.

I have been instructed on how to properly sort them, put them into their little specimen containers, mark the caps with the proper times and take them on my own. Initially it was confusing with this large variety of pills but what makes it much more difficult is that my hands shake so much from the medication. It looks and feels like I'm freezing uncontrollably and I can't stop. I can barely get the little cellophane packets each pill comes in open and then drop that darn pill into its' proper container. It's so bad I have to ask the nurse to help me open the cellophane packets or it will take a ridiculous amount of time to complete this simple task. I'm not complaining, I'm just saying it's difficult. After three long, tough weeks in the hospital I met with my post-transplant doctor and simply said, "At this point, I think I will recover faster out of the hospital than in it". I had been told by my doctors for over a week now that I would be discharged any day. Unfortunately they always kept me in, mostly because my kidneys were not kicking in and functioning properly. Surprisingly though, today, December 16, approximately one month after my surgery they were all in agreement and after conferring with the other doctors who were caring for my various issues I was able to "go home". I left with my Foley intact and now had a small Foley bag that was strapped onto my leg. I could easily empty this bag on my own. This was the first time I felt like I was going to actually ever leave this hospital alive. My IV was taken out, the IV pump and pole were disconnected and another draining tube was pulled out of my chest. My heart monitors were all taken off and I felt like a huge burden had been taken away. I was able to wear underwear finally, and with the small Foley bag I was able to put on pants. Pants! I had just one more chest draining tube left. I was on my way to living a normal life once again.

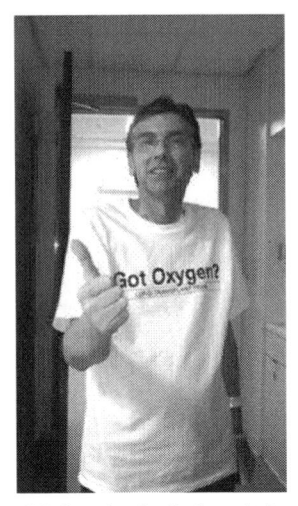

My last day in the hospital.

I remember going outside for the first time into the cold air and thinking back one month earlier when I was wondering if I would ever experience this feeling again. Well, I should have listened to my wife, because she never had any doubt I would.

Going home of course actually meant a "suites" hotel that Deb had been staying at, well, sleeping at, but it was another step up in comfort and privacy.

I was now administering my own meds., taking my own blood pressure, checking on my lung function with a portable spirometer that every patient uses after transplant and Deb was changing my bandages of the remaining chest tube I had in place. We walked up and down the hotel hallways to build my strength, went to Target and Borders, me with a surgical mask on and ordered out from the many restaurants that dotted the area. The bed at that hotel was like sleeping on a cloud, I understood why Deb would like to leave me after a long day at Cleveland Clinic. She could sink into that bed and relax, and I don't blame her. I was still very unsteady and weak on my feet and used a walker at times. I fell, I think on my second day in the hotel. That was OK, but the hard part was I couldn't get up. Deb was out of the room and she found me on the floor. I had to drag myself over to a chair and use it as leverage to lift myself up off the floor. I couldn't believe how difficult a normally easy thing like getting off the floor was.

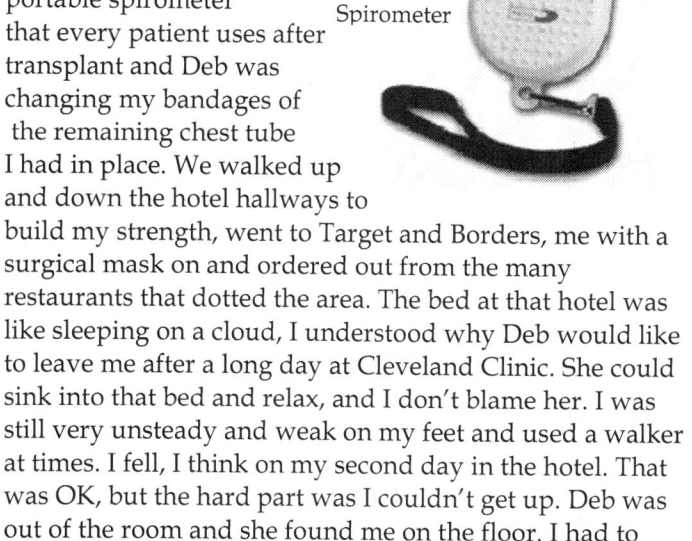

Mikaela came down on the first weekend I was out, and although she had seen me once in the hospital, I looked much more like dad, in street clothes and minus any visible tubes. I think it put her more at ease and allowed her to know that I was going to be OK. I was finally able to wash my hair and body, not in a shower but leaning over the tub and letting the shower wash over my greasy,

Portable Spirometer

unwashed hair. The only "medical" appointment was for blood work which I was able to have taken at a nearby satellite hospital during that week at the hotel.

On December 22nd I had my first post-transplant appointment with my doctors. My stitches were removed that held in my remaining chest tube, the tube was pulled, the incision stitched up and I did my first post PFT's (pulmonary function tests).

Everything went great and I was officially granted an honorable discharge from Cleveland Clinic on December 22nd. It had been just over one month since my surgery. Deb and I were thrilled. We would be home for the Christmas holiday. Although I didn't personally celebrate the Christmas holiday any longer, my family still did with my mother and sisters. I was excited to be going back home again. The drive home from Cleveland was uneventful, three hours from Cleveland to Buffalo can be harrowing, but that day the drive was nice, dry and relaxing. The drive home was a feeling I will never forget. It seemed like the world was a different place to me now. I was going home but no longer worrying if my oxygen tank was going to last and no longer worrying about how I was constantly feeling. I wasn't coughing at all anymore, so strange, so odd.

I have always felt odd walking into my home after my lengthy hospital stays. It almost feels like I'm walking into someone else's home. It seems like a new experience each time, even though I live there. Coming home from Cleveland was no exception. It takes a little while to get comfortable in my own home. This time though the comfort level was at an all-time high. I had no problem walking or breathing or performing any of the tasks that would normally exhaust me. This was a feeling I can easily get used to!

My Daily Medications

The medications I am now on are extremely strong and they do crazy things to your body. The long term negative effects the medications have on the kidneys and liver are a necessary evil. But besides all that I had issues such as ridiculous uncontrollable shaking. For a time I could not write a sentence or sign my name because my hands shook so much. My whole body would shake when I was still or lying down and it was hard to concentrate on

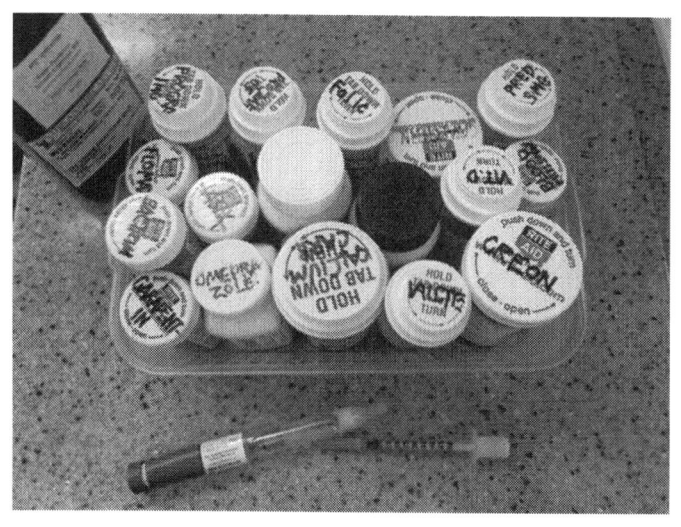

These medications I take on a daily basis except for the bottle in the back left (SPS), which I take once a week. The injection pen on the left is Humalog, on the right is a syringe for Lantus.

just falling asleep. I was also extremely emotional. I would cry about anything or nothing and feel an extreme sense of desperation and depression. It was a feeling of hopelessness in a world full of promise. My face always has this swollen look to it from the steroids. In the hospital I had the "moon face" effect really severe and my face was very round. Now it is better, but still an issue. For a while I was on a medication that made my hair fall out. It was not a noticeable problem to anyone else, but when I took a shower I could see what was happening in my hand or on my washcloth My doctors, although sympathetic to the issues I was going through were limited what they could do. They understood the problems because time and time again another person would come to them and complain about the same things or other similar side effects. For a few medications they were able to switch them out with another, most however, had to stay as they were. Today I still have the shaking although it is much, much better and my hair just stopped coming out one day, my hair is the last vestige of my former youth so I am very thankful for that and apparently my body has learned to tolerate the medications better. I take my medications mostly twice a day. 8 am and 8 pm, with a few minor variations with some others. Today I take Prograf for rejection, Prednisone for rejection, Zithromax for bacterial infection, Bactrim for bacterial infection, Noxafil for fungal infection, Valcyte for viral infections, Metoprolol Tartrate for blood pressure, Folic Acid for nutrition, a Multivitamin for nutrition, Vitamin D for bone strength, Flomax for an enlarged prostate, Lasix for water retention, Gabapentin for nerve pain, Omeprazole for heartburn, Calcium Carbonate for low calcium level, Sodium Polystyrene Sulfate(SPS) for high potassium, Lantus for blood sugar, Humalog for blood sugar and a few other various medications for, well… other things. I have just recently been taken off of Fosamax for bone density. I had taken Fosamax for around

10 years and my most recent DexaScan showed improved results, so at least temporarily, I am off that medication.

I have taken many, many different medications over the last several years, but the one's I take today for my double lung transplant are by far the most important and I don't miss or skip a dosage.

I have heard from my doctors that some people who have had transplants stop taking their medications because they feel their health is good enough to discontinue their prescribed medications. I cannot express enough to a person in this type of situation just how important it is to NOT STOP taking a medication prescribed to them. It truly is a matter of life and death. With these immune suppressing medications I am much more susceptible to other illness such as colds or influenza or who knows what else. Life is sometimes a roll of the dice to use a common metaphor, but it's certainly worth the gamble.

A Life Changer   January, 2010

   I know I may be repeating myself, but I cannot express the anxiety and fear I felt about this huge life challenge I was not only already in, but was about to take on. Look, cystic fibrosis is a deadly serious disease. It doesn't go away, it doesn't get better. It stays with you and slowly destroys your body. Everyone is different when it comes to CF. There are many different levels and different gene mutations of this disease. I went through some tough times, but...I don't think I can really put into words how this transplant has *improved* my life.

   I believe that the many young people and adults with CF will feel that a double lung transplant is a potential death sentence. I know I felt that way going in. I felt that it was the last final attempt to save what was left of my life and it was being done not to return me to a fulfilling life but to a different stage before death. Perhaps a slightly better, more tolerable, easier to live with period before the end. Sure I was told by my CF doctors I would be a much happier, healthier individual with the transplant, but really, I wasn't so sure. I did not know much about the transplantation process nor did anyone teach me or instruct me on what to expect before, during or after the surgery. This is one aspect of the transplant dialogue I would change. The education of transplantation, for me anyway, was simply not there. These CF people need to know what's going to happen and what to expect. They need to talk with fellow CF'ers who have gone through this surgery. They need to know that everything is going to be OK and they are going to experience a kind of medical miracle, a transformation in their bodies that will change their lives for the better. They need a better education in lung transplantation besides the internet or a book or a pamphlet.

   My quality of life has increased exponentially. What I

can say is: I've regained an appetite that I had lost so long ago I didn't even remember what it was like to have one. Food used to make me nauseous just to look at, now I eat too much of it. I have gained almost 30 pounds. I regained the ability to walk again without being exhausted. When I have an appointment at Cleveland Clinic I walk over from the Guest House to the Cleveland Clinic now. I don't need to take that shuttle bus any more. I don't need that wheelchair anymore. Walking was completely lost to me prior to transplant. I sleep in a bed once more. I had not slept in a bed in probably three or four years. I also sleep lying down, FLAT, on my back. That took some time getting used to again. I can exercise. Like jog, ride a bike, use an elliptical exercise machine. I don't do my vest anymore. That means no more chest PT. That routine lasted 10 years, twice a day or more for thirty minutes each session. That comes out to approximately 3,650 hours or 152 days! I don't use any more inhalers. No ibuterol, no TOBI, no saline, no DNase. I don't use liquid oxygen at all. I used it continually prior to transplant. No more nutritional supplements. That routine although necessary, was exhausting, and I must say, it's darn nice not having a feeding tube and "button" coming out of my stomach anymore. I don't cough anymore. My wife had only known me coughing. That is a huge change not only for me but my entire family and everyone that knows me.

But with this life changing gift I also now do things to avoid getting infections and germs that could result in a cold or the seasonal flu. That could result in a very negative outcome. I am on anti-rejection medications and my immune system will always be compromised. That means the chances of getting a cold are far greater than they once were. So I avoid crowds, specifically movie theatres, churches and temples or crowded restaurants. These are a no-no. I have and will attend necessary religious services and dining engagements but try to avoid them when I believe it's compromising to my health. I am always aware of the people around me at my daughters choral or theatre events and have and will move to another seat if I feel it is necessary for my health. Although it may seem foolish to go to such lengths to maintain my health, I know it is not. I also know that others with similar situations do the same. It is a small price to pay to live the quality of life I live today. It is not perfect, with the good comes some bad, but it is a good compromise and I am not complaining.

I don't have much feeling on the right side of my chest now since my transplant, and that is a bit odd. Apparently many nerves are severed during surgery. I was told this could occur and that it may or may not ever return. I also have scars in a number of places on my torso with the most obvious one traveling armpit to armpit. My muscle definition in my chest is no longer what it once was. These are all somewhat negative results of my chest being opened during transplant of my new lungs, but these negatives will never outweigh the huge positive I have received with my new lungs.

Yes, I still have cystic fibrosis. My lung transplant didn't change that. I was born with this disease and I will die with it. Very possibly, I will die from a complication of it. I still have major issues with my pancreas and diabetes. I still have cirrhosis of the liver. But hey, we all have to die from something, be it heart disease, cancer, getting struck by lightning or cystic fibrosis. Unlike most however, I have been given a second chance to live.

I have kept many of the drugs and medications I used daily before my transplant. It is my reminder of a past that was full of time consuming rituals for continued health. I often look at these medications sitting on a shelf or in a drawer and remember the necessity of them at that point in my life. I choose to never forget that time, not because it was memorable, it was not, but because it was so difficult and I never want to forget where I've come from.

   I believe if a person with CF reads what I have just conveyed they will realize that this immovable obstacle of reliance to these grueling daily routines and this crutch of struggling to survive can be removed from their life. I'm not saying it will be easy, or even possible for all. But if the option is available the unimaginable potential of discarding that existence, an existence that prevents them from really living, can be thrown away. This opportunity can be a life changer. And life changing opportunities don't come around very often.

My First Visit Back to Cleveland
January 5, 2010

I have my first return visit to Cleveland since the transplant. I go through my usual procedure of Labs, X-Ray, PFT's and Doctor visit. We discuss among other things my shakes, my emotional swings and depression. I am told these are all typical symptoms of patients on these medications and I'm told if they don't subside I can go to specialists for my emotional issues. I decline that advice for now. The shakes I will probably always have to some degree I am told. My PFT's are good however, my FEV1 is 90%, and my FVC is 72%. Should I repeat that… FEV1 -90%, FVC - 72%. My pulseox. is 100%! They do however spot a shadow in my lower chest area and I am sent to have an ultrasound done. The ultrasound reveals fluid in my chest cavity and while I'm having the ultrasound the technician marks two areas on the back side of my chest with a marker. A kind of "X" marks the spot. My draining tubes have all been removed at this point, so the fluid that has accumulated has nowhere to go, it just collects in my chest cavity and now must be drained. Ugh, I think, what are they going to do to me now? Well, I find out soon enough as Dr. Olbrych decides he's going to drain it right there and then during my usual office visit. I trust Dr. Olbrych completely and he does not let me down. Although there is fluid on both sides he feels it is safest to do just my right side as it is worse. He asks me to lean over the examining table, then he numbs my chest directly behind my right arm. He inserts a needle between my ribs and into my chest cavity and begins suctioning out the excess light yellowish liquid. He's able to extract about one liter of fluid. It's doesn't take him more than 5 minutes, although from my standpoint it feels much, much longer. The pain was minimal, and I have gotten used to pain in some form or other by now.

My final appointment of the day is with the urologist. We discuss my Foley situation which was still in and empting my blatter. I am against taking it out at this point because I would have to wait around the clinic until I urinate, at which time they would let me go home. I want to have it pulled back in Buffalo. My doctor agreed and my day was done.

I head back to Buffalo relieved, relieved for the first time in almost five years.

My Benefit   February, 2010

Shown is a portion of the dedicated staff at the Lung and Cystic Fibrosis Center of Women and Children's Hospital of Buffalo. Seated on the left is Dr. Drucy Borowitz, Director of the Cystic Fibrosis Center and seated to the right Dr. Michael Aronica, Adult Program Director.
I'm the tall one in the middle holding the plaque.

My neighbors (Erin, Deter, Colleen, Joe, Betsy, Kathi and Rob) have been planning a benefit for me to raise money for our various expenses. It is an extreme gesture of kindness and compassion for not only me but my family. Tickets have been sold and just prior to the benefit which is being held at Rob's Comedy Playhouse the event is sold out. It is an amazing expression of caring from all the people who were concerned enough to purchase tickets and donate their time and money to a benefit that is for me. I don't feel I deserve such attention, I do however appreciate it.

I have decided to donate a portion of the proceeds from my benefit to the Lung and Cystic Fibrosis Center at

WCHOB. The money is going for items directly relating to the 10th floor, and the cystic patients who spend so much of their time receiving treatment in this unit. I think about them often and wish them all well.

Although the bulk of my expenses have been paid for with our comprehensive health insurance, the cost of Deborah being in a hotel for a month and the obvious various costs associated with being away from home for such a long period of time do add up.

I recently received my bill from Cleveland Clinic for the surgery and hospital stay. The cost of my surgery and hospital stay, including my various tests, blood work and procedures not including the many tests that have been performed throughout these past 4 years exceeded $500,000.00 Personally I'm thrilled, not so much about the exorbitant cost but by the amazing results.

I recently have been going to respiratory therapy to build up my lung strength, endurance and my muscle tone, I walk daily on my treadmill at home and although I am often tired and don't feel like myself, I know I am getting better. I was told to expect a recovery of up to 1 year so I know that a month and half out from transplant is still no time at all. I am looking forward to 2010 and beyond because really, how many people can say they have been given the gift of life, really another chance at life. WOW!

Rejection #1   February-March, 2010

Every week on a Monday morning I leave my home and head to the local diagnostic lab for weekly blood work. I walk in wearing a surgical mask, (to guard against germs) and carry a UPS bag which contains a small shipping box, 3 lab vials, a blood lab request form and labels for the vials. A total of 5 vials of blood are taken weekly and three are sent to Cleveland for processing. Two are processed here in Buffalo and the results are forwarded to Cleveland.

I receive a call from my Post Transplant Coordinator; Mike, usually on Wednesday or Thursday with my results. He will usually give me the OK and I will continue to take my medications with no changes or perhaps he'll tell me to adjust my Prograf (anti-rejection) medication slightly, usually a half milligram plus or minus.

Today however he gives me news I was not entirely prepared for. My lungs were going through slight rejection. The thing that amazes me about this whole process is he is so matter of fact about it. He seems to be treating it like it's no big deal. I'm in a bit of shock, to me it's a big deal! I think back to Dr. Budev telling me during my last few pre-transplant appointments to expect rejection. She told me it was common and happened to the majority of transplant recipients. Still, I was hoping I could beat the odds. So now I know I could not.

I am instructed to increase my steroid medication and I will be seen in Cleveland in a month. I'm listed as a Level 1 rejection, not a major rejection issue but still any form of rejection must be taken seriously.

A UPS package with my appointment schedule comes to my front door in two days, my appointment in Cleveland is scheduled for March, 11. The date cannot come soon enough.

In Cleveland I go through the usual routine of Lab work, X-Ray, but this time an Ultrasound is listed on the appointment schedule, then PFT's, doctors appointment and then a bronchoscopy at 11:30am. After the chest X-ray I have my ultrasound and they again find a shadow in my chest. I know this without asking because again the ultrasound technician puts an "X" on my back. This is the spot they will drain my excess fluid from.

   My doctor today is Dr. Budev. She has me do my bronchoscopy first and then come back to the Crile Building and have the fluid drained out of my chest cavity. A biopsy is taken of my lung tissue during the bronchoscopy and the left lung is inspected for rejection. The doctor who performs my chest fluid draining doesn't do a spectacular job and the pain is challenging to tolerate. I go home tired and sore but better than when I came. I'm happy it's over. What a day!

Rejection # 2   May 21, 2010

The scare from the first rejection had subsided. I was called about a week after my last visit to Cleveland and told the rejection was medicinally corrected and I need not worry any longer. I didn't. It was now May and everything was going well. I felt good and was doing my blood pressure and Spirometry each morning and evening. There would be times my FEV1 or FVC will go down but it always seemed to bounce back up after a week or so. The second week in May my numbers stayed down and I thought maybe my Spirometer wasn't working properly. I had my blood work done as usual on Monday. I got the call early in the day on a Thursday. Mike, the Post-Transplant Coordinator gave me the news that my lungs were in rejection once more. This was a Level 2 rejection. The rejection scale goes 1 to 4 so although it was not the worst it needed immediate attention. It's the oddest feeling getting a call like that. The lungs in my body, a major component in keeping me alive, we not happy in their home and wanted to rebel. They wanted to move out, but my doctors weren't going to let them. It's scary to know this and scary wondering if it will get worse or be medically corrected and get better.

   This rejection required IV steroids, something I had not had during my first rejection. Within a day or two an IV was placed in my arm by a visiting nurse and for three days I received 550 MG of Solu-Medrol 1GM A-O-V, the "mega" dose of steroids. After the three days I was taken off the "mega" dose but took a larger dose of steroids orally.

   I was again told I would be seen in Cleveland in approximately a month. The morning of my appointment I decide to walk over from the Guest House instead of take the shuttle. What a thrill that walk was. During my appointment I had my third broncoscopy. Dr. Olbrych performs the procedure and again a tissue sample was taken this time of the right lung. I was given pictures of the bronchial "tree" to both lungs. Amazingly you can clearly see the treads where both lungs are attached to the bronchial tubes. Kind of creepy, kind of scary, kind of amazing.

Another appointment is made for a month. A broncoscopy is scheduled during this appointment just in case I need further and more aggressive treatment. My biopsy will determine that. About a week and a half later I received the results that my lungs were good to go. Whew! I don't care what anyone says about rejection medication and its ability to fool the body into accepting a foreign object, you simply never know what's going to happen or when.

I've had my PEG removed. That damn protrusion is no longer sticking out of my stomach. I hated that thing. Sometimes it would get irritated or infected and it hurt like a bitch to touch. That made it difficult to attach the PEG tube to my PEG button as you had to push into the button to snap it on. I can still remember that pain like it was yesterday. I had the procedure to remove it done at an outpatient center. I was taken into an out-patient prep area. Everyone was lined up on their gurneys, a white curtain separating us, each getting prepped for their various procedure. My doctor came in and made a crack about how I was going to have two bellybuttons now. I asked him how my PEG removal was going to be performed and he said, "It will be a simple tug and it will be out". I wanted to know how that could happen since I knew there is a stopper in my stomach from it falling out in the first place. My doctor told me I did not need to ask any more questions and if I did he would not even perform the procedure at all. I stated to him that I just wanted to know what was going to happen and that's when he put his one hand on my stomach at the insertion point of the PEG, grabbed the end of the PEG and pulled. It was like a cork coming out of a wine bottle. It hurt like hell coming out and then it was over. Maybe it was best I didn't know what was going to happen, but I decided then and there I was not going to ever use him again for any follow-up procedures, (he had done both my colonoscopies too). Unfortunately my opinion of him was diminished greatly following that procedure, but at least it's out.

The insertion point eventually heals with no special treatment or medication, but you do have what looks like a hole or second bellybutton in your stomach. I often felt like they should cosmetically fix that, but with all the scars I have on my chest I guess another visual imperfection in my appearance doesn't matter. It's not like I'm going to go swimming with my shirt off anymore anyway and trying to impress the girls.

I'm Not a Hero

My wife has said that I am her hero because of my lung transplant. Yes, it does take inner strength and courage with what I have experienced, not only the transplant, but the life of having cystic fibrosis, but I know many, many other people who have, are and will go through much worse times than I. Perhaps they are the hero's in this crazy world, and I wish them all well.

I believe almost any person who has served our country in the military is a hero in the sense that they knowingly have volunteered to put their lives on the line especially in times of war so you and I can live in this free country. Perhaps they are the hero's in this crazy world.

An acquaintance of mine, Nancy Matthews has written two books. One is about how to deal with a chronic or terminal illness and the other is more about her life. It is more spiritual and deals with life's ups and downs. Nancy Matthews also has cystic fibrosis and has had her own double lung transplant. She is presently working as a volunteer for Donate Life, an organization which among other things teaches the need and importance of organ donation. There could not be a better spokesperson. She is a dynamic, strong and interesting person to listen to and to meet. Nancy is dedicated to helping others in her post-transplant life. Nancy Matthews is *giving* when she could be receiving. She is far closer to being a hero than I could ever be. Perhaps she is a hero in this crazy world.

The one thing I know for sure is I'm not a hero.

A Belief in Something Greater

When you have an experience like a double lung transplant or another serious situation in your life I believe you naturally do what you hope or believe will help… you pray to G-d. How many times have you said to yourself "Please G-d help me through this. If such and such happens and everything turns out OK, I promise I will always go to church or I will always go to temple or I'll treat my family better or eat all my vegetables", you get what I mean. I believe being a religious person truly helps those in need. Maybe not physically, but certainly spiritually and emotionally.

I recently was looking at a book my daughter was reading. In it was an explanation of G-d which I thought was very appropriate and realistic. It said that G-d is not a person or the moon, sun or stars. G-d is not a great king. G-d is the good that's in the world. And he made everything. I believe most of this is true. I'm not entirely sure of the usage of the word "he", nor am I entirely sure of the sentence that he made everything. I'm not saying no to this, I'm just not saying yes to it. I often wonder why G-d does not make itself available to us in a physical sense, like apparently he did thousands of years ago, say to Moses. When I was extremely sick I prayed to G-d because looking back on it today, it made me feel better. I know in my heart that there was no G-d listening to my prayers, absorbing my thoughts and taking them into consideration. I knew G-d was not going to decide my fate. If I was going to die, it was not because G-d felt it "was my time". I was going to die because of some situation in this complicated process that was unexpected, maybe the new lungs didn't take to their new host, or maybe my kidneys would fail or I would get an infection that could not be corrected.

If there is a G-d that does actually listen to people's

problems and needs I think it would do a much better job of curing them of their illness or relieving them of their pain. I believe G-d is more an emotional and spiritual release and a personal reassurance that there is something greater and better out there. What I mean by greater is the power of your *own* inner strength and fortitude to get through a crisis as best as *you're* able.

Sometime after my surgery my wife said to me "Thank G-d that he got you through this surgery and made you healthy again". I thought about that for just a second and commented. "If there is a G-d, I would thank him for giving my surgeons the great ability to know how to successfully perform such a complicated operation and bring me out of it alive". I don't believe G-d had anything to do with me living through that critical surgery and post-surgery trauma but I do believe maybe if there is a G-d that he gave my caregivers the knowledge to implement the proper care for my successful recovery. G-d was not there overseeing my progress and making sure I was going to make it through the surgery OK.

Many may disagree with this belief and call that an atheist view. I don't believe that I am. I also don't believe that people who believe G-d is with them at every step of their life are wrong to do so. I just believe we are often at the mercy of our physical surrounding environment. We can however, impact our own spiritual and emotional position or environment by our inner faith in G-d or by our need and ability to pray to G-d.

My father-in-law is what I would call a spiritual person. He regularly goes to temple often many times a week, always on Saturday, the Sabbath. He has always attended all holy days for the required periods as he was raised to unless he was of course sick with an illness. I believe he is right for doing all this, I believe it makes him feel content with himself and his religious beliefs. I know he has prayed for me when he was in temple. I believe this helped in my recovery, but I don't believe G-d specifically was listening to him and granting him his prayer of good health and wellness for me.

Regardless of my perhaps religiously unconventional beliefs I will still pray to G-d when I feel it is spiritually comforting to me. That is what I understand and that is what I believe and it is what I do.

Unyts and Donate Life

I don't think most people are aware of the Donate Life organization. "Donate Life America is a not-for-profit alliance of national organizations and state teams across the United States committed to increasing organ, eye and tissue donation. Donate Life America manages and promotes the national brand for donation, Donate Life, and assists Donate Life State Teams and national partners in facilitating high-performing donor registries; developing and executing effective multi-media donor education programs; and motivating the American public to register now as organ, eye and tissue donors. What this simply means is Donate Life promotes the awareness, recognition and registry of organ donors."[6] Donate Life has State Teams that work to promote organ donation.

Unyts (Upstate New York Transplant Services) operates in downtown Buffalo as a non-profit serving the eight counties of Western New York and works to assist donor families, Unyts is among the leading procurement organizations in the United States, and is one of the only eight centers nationwide to house laboratory services, and organ, tissue and eye procurement in one location.

With the addition of Community Blood Services, Unyts has become the first organization of its kind nationwide.

The blood collected in Western New York stays right in the immediate community.

"Unyts routinely has helped to secure higher rates of donation in Western New York than the national average. When approached following the death of a loved-one for organ donation, Western New York families give consent nearly 90% – the national average is roughly 60%. Due to this generosity, Unyts has ranked in the top ten procurement organizations nationwide in terms of rates of consent for seven of the past eight years."[14]

My wife Deborah who is a business teacher at the high school level has worked closely with Unyts and the Donate Life organization for several years to promote and educate young people on the value of organ and tissue donation. Each year she sets aside a portion of her Youth Leadership class specifically on this topic. My wife has done this out of love for me and the belief that another's untimely demise can open the door of life giving opportunity to another. I thank her for this and I thank Donate Life. I have worn a Donate Life wrist band (they are green) every day since my transplant to promote this life saving organization.

One Year Anniversary   November, 2010

I'm celebrating my one year anniversary. Soon we will be in the height of the holiday season. Deb and I are having a holiday party this year. We have always had a Hanukkah party with some neighbors and friends, however last year we did not as I was in the hospital and Deborah was there with me. And last year I was released from the hospital to the hotel during the 8 days of Hanukkah so Deb and I celebrated with paper candles on a paper menorah. This year we will be at home celebrating with a real menorah and real candles.

Recently my daughter Mikaela told me that it took some getting used to having her father home and a part of the family once again. She said it felt odd and awkward with me around and participating in daily family activities. She was actually used to me at a hospital more than at home and if I was home I was always in a chair or in a room with my oxygen on.

I never thought my illness made this kind of an impact on my daughter. It's amazing how this illness has impacted her life. When she was a baby I would stand next to her crib while she was sleeping and worry I would not see her at this age (10 years). I really believed I was cheating her out of having a father and apparently for a while I was. Today I no longer "cheat" her and today we are able to do so much more together. She gets her father's attention and love 110% now. This opportunity has given me such a reward. It has been one year since I have been admitted to a hospital. I haven't gone this long not being in a hospital since 2001, which is about nine years.

A Letter to My Donors Family and Loved Ones

February 1, 2011

On November 19th, 2009 I was given a miraculous gift. It was the gift of life. For me to live, unfortunately another has died. This is why I am writing to you today.
Not only to thank you and express my gratitude for this great opportunity to live but also to express my sincere condolences for the loss of your loved one.
I cannot imagine what you have gone through and the pain you have endured, it is not something to be forgotten and when I think of my gift I also think of your loss.
I do not know you, I do not know anything about my donor, but I do know their life has not ended in their untimely death. They certainly live on in me and for this I am forever grateful. I have a disease called Cystic Fibrosis. The disease destroyed my lungs and prior to November 19th, they were functioning at about 15% of their capacity.
I was on constant oxygen and could not do anything but sit in a chair and watch my life ebb away. My daughter was nine at the time and I was barely a part of her young world, I could only watch as she grew up without me.

Today I have a beautifully functioning pair of lungs. I don't use or need additional oxygen and have a quality of life that I had forgotten existed. My wife, daughter and I have done things as a family we could not have done prior to receiving my gift and each day I wake up with the great miracle of what my life has become.

Thank you again and my generous donor for the life they gave me, the husband they gave back to my wife and the father they gave back to my daughter.

Sincerely,

William Mahaney

I sent this letter of thanks and condolence to the donor family one year after my double lung transplant. I am not allowed to respond to the donor family until the first anniversary of my transplant. I never received a reply back. It is the donor families or spouses discretion to respond to a letter from the donor recipient. Some respond with a letter, some respond and eventually meet the transplant recipient, some choose to do nothing.

The Ability to Walk Again   October, 2011

My mother has recently been in the hospital for a heart condition. As we were driving past the hospital she had been admitted to I was telling my wife how far away I had to park from the hospital entrance because the lot was always so full.

"Why didn't you just use the valet service" she asked? "It's so much easier". It was a quick answer for me. "For me, it's a privilege to be able to walk, I spent so many years needing the valet service that now I prefer to walk and experience the feeling of being able to do it myself" I said. "That's good" said my wife, now aware that such a simple accomplishment would mean so much to me, and then we went on to something else.

I don't think she ever really thought that way about walking before, but when you can't do something, especially when you were able to at some point in your life, it's a real eye opener, and you learn to appreciate those things much more. I know I mentioned this walking issue earlier and what a pain in the ass it was to be so limited. It's true however and it is a big deal to not have to agonize with the problem any longer.

Remember when you see a person in a wheel chair that there is a myriad of reasons for them being there, and really try, I mean *really try* not to judge or dissect their reason for being in that position, because you just never know when you could be in that situation at some point in your life also.

My Two Year Anniversary   November 19, 2011

I got my hair cut today. I drove to the salon Jenny works at. She no longer has to come to me. I put up a hand rail going two steps down into our mudroom. I attempted to put up Hanukkah lights but half of them were not working. I will have to buy more soon. I went to Lowe's and bought a few small odds and ends. Tonight I'm having dinner with the two people I love more than anything in this world. I won't be exhausted after all this. I won't need to sit in a chair and dread getting out of it. I won't consider "all this" too much. I will live the life I thought about for so long.

It has been two years since I last used my vest. It is in the hall closet. TWO YEARS. That vest was a big part of my daily routine for almost ten years.

I still avoid crowds or groups of people but I'm living a much more normal life. Today is my two year anniversary of my double lung transplant surgery. Haircut, Hanukkah lights, dinner with my family. These are the things I am grateful for. These are the things I would not be doing if not for my gift of two healthy lungs. Thank you again to my donor. I am sorry for your loss of life, I am thankful for your giving of life. I know I am always in danger of rejection. I have heard a transplant typically lasts two years. I choose not to think about it. It could happen tomorrow or it could happen in 10 years from tomorrow. I am as prepared as a person in this situation can be. Every day is a gift. I know that.

Thanks to All

I would be remiss not to thank all the people who sent me cards, flowers, fruit baskets, monetary donations, those who were able to visit me in Cleveland, called and prayed for me. EVERY SINGLE ONE OF YOU made me feel better, this is not a clique, but what I found to be very powerful in my healing and recovery process.

Thanks of course to my family for all their love and support, especially my wife Deborah. I could not have gotten through that difficult time without her by my side. Thanks to my daughter Mikaela who in many respects I lived for. There is nothing in this world that made me fight more to live than her. Thanks to my in-laws, Daniel and Ida. I couldn't have asked for more support from them. It was always a comfort for me to know they would be there for us, to help where they could, when they could. It took a lot of stress off me knowing Deb and Mikaela were in their loving hands. Although my brother and sister in-law, David and Donna could not physically be here to offer their assistance because they live in Long Island, I know, just the same, they were there if we needed them. Again that burden of "what if "was relieved just by knowing they were there just in case. Dana, my sister in-law, Deb's twin, was incredibly helpful, especially when I was at the Cleveland Clinic. She became a part time mom, and although sometimes she was exhausted and stressed from the amount of work and time a child takes, she never said "no" or "I can't.". Thanks for all that Dana and thanks to ALL my family for ALL you've done for me.

Thanks to Dr. Joseph Cronin, my CF doctor at WCHOB, who addressed my disease with a fight to win attitude. He was always ready to try a little harder, dig a little deeper and fight a little longer, and honestly as much as I at times disliked it, I cannot thank him enough for his dedication. I trusted him with my life, literally and figuratively.

Dr. Cronin is a brilliant man, and behind most great doctors are strong support people. Lynn Fries, PA and Jeanne Smith, RN, CPN were both there to administer, advise, befriend and support me in my long days and weeks at WCHOB. And thanks to Maureen "Moe" Stewart who is not only an excellent nurse on the CF floor, but a great friend as well. I cannot forget Cindy Brown, another excellent nurse and Dale Pawarski, also a superb nurse and Joe Nesarajah, the most compassionate, dedicated respiratory therapist I could ask for. And thanks to Kim Rand, Chris Colburn-Miller, Sandy Prentice, Sally Raskin, and Barbara Howard. All dedicated people and out-standing in their profession.

And thanks to all the incredibly talented professional personnel at Cleveland Clinic. This includes the nurses who have a job that requires incredible patience and compassion. Thanks to the doctors, P.A.'s, phlebotomists, X-Ray technicians, dialysis personnel, ultrasound technicians, clergy and numerous other Cleveland Clinic personnel who supported me during this difficult period. Special thanks to Marie Budev, DO and Thomas Olbrych., MD. These two doctors in particular have guided me through the pre-transplant and post-transplant process with incredible compassion, knowledge and professionalism and gave me the courage to move forward when I really wanted to stand still. And of course thanks to David P. Mason, MD my transplant surgeon who I literally owe my life to, and all those involved in the actual transplant surgery. Dr. Mason was always incredibly sympathetic to my situation and listened and answered all of my questions and concerns. Thanks also to my primary transplant coordinator Mike Cwalina, who is always watching over me, even when I'm not at the Cleveland Clinic. All these people and many, many others have made my life worth living once again. That is not just an empty phrase either, it is the honest truth. THANK YOU ALL.

The End of My Story, but Not My Fight

I sincerely hope that most or perhaps all of your questions about cystic fibrosis have been answered in story. It is not always an easy disease to understand, it is not always an easy disease to live with, but it is a disease that with greater knowledge and greater advances in medicine can be controlled and maybe, just maybe someday can be cured.

"The FDA recently approved a drug called Kalydeco that has proved effective in treating CF patients with the G551D mutation. The drug helps the protein made by the CFTR gene function better and as a result, improves lung function and other aspects of CF such as increasing weight gain. Approximately 4% of the CF population have the G551D mutation. Various other drug are being tested for the most common gene mutation, F508."[15]

For more information on cystic fibrosis, explore the library or the internet. There are dozens of excellent books and websites on the subject today. Visit cff.org the official website of the Cystic Fibrosis Foundation if you would like to donate your time or money to this worthy foundation or to become more educated on the disease .

I believe my life has been an adventure. An adventure of desperation, promise, love, hope, belief, opportunity and a bit of luck. I know many people experience serious and painful illness. It unfortunately happens every day in every part of this world. My illness is certainly not the worst you have ever read about, it is not the most tragic, it is not the most unusual, it is not the most unfortunate. Many people have gone through far worse than I. This is simply the life of one man, one individual of 70,000 on this planet with an illness called cystic fibrosis.

This photo was taken during the winter holidays 2011. Pictured are my wife Deborah, myself and my daughter Mikaela. Honestly each and every day that I can open my eyes, get up out of bed and spend with my family I view as a sort of miracle. I know in my heart that the day will be, no matter the circumstances, a day to be thankful for.

Abbreviations

CAT scan – Computerized Axial Tomography scan

CF - Cystic Fibrosis

CFRD – Cystic Fibrosis Related Diabetes

COPD- Chronic Obstructive Pulmonary Disease

ICU - Intensive Care Unit

IV – Intravenous

FDA – U.S. Food and Drug Administration

FEV1 - Forced Expiratory Volume in 1 second

FVC - Forced Vital Capacity

O2 – Oxygen

OR – Operating Room

PFT – Pulmonary Function Test

PEG – Percutaneous Endoscopic Gastrostomy

PICC - Peripherally Inserted Central Catheter

PT – Physical Therapy

UNYTS – Upstate New York Transplant Services

Vest - The Vest Airway Clearance System

WCHOB – Women & Children's Hospital of Buffalo

Resources

1. Alma, Lori. "About Us: Cystic Fibrosis." 21 July 2009. *Cystic Fibrosis.* 30 August 2012.
   <http://cysticfibrosis.about.com/od/cysticfibrosis101/f/CFcarrier.htm>.

2. "About Us: Cystic Fibrosis." 08 October 2008. *Cystic Fibrosis–Related Diabetes.* 30 August 2012.
   <http://cysticfibrosis.about.com/od/relateddiseases/a/CFRD.htm>.

3. al, Fathi et. "Cough." 18 January 2009. *BioMed Central Ltd.* . 30 August 2012. <http://www.coughjournal.com/content/5/1/1/>.

4. *Cystic Fibrosis Canada.* 19 August 2009. 30 August 2012.
   <http://cysticfibrosis.ca/en/aboutCysticFibrosis/NasalPolyps.php>.

5. Damry, Damry. *Helium, Inc.* n.d. 30 August 2012.
   <http://disease.helium.com/topic/7897-digestive-enzymes>.

6. *Donate Life America.* n.d. 30 August 2012.
   <http://donatelife.net/about-us/>.

7. Lang, Constance. *ehow: A Demand Media Property.* n.d. 30 August 2012.
   <http://www.ehow.com/how-does_4963808_bipap-machine-work.html>.

8. *Wikipedia.* 6 May 2012 . 30 August 2012.
   <http://en.wikipedia.org/wiki/Cardiac_catheterization>.

9. *Wikipedia.* 31 August 2012. 30 August 2012.
   <http://en.wikipedia.org/wiki/Cystic_fibrosis>.

10. *Wikipedia.* 7 August 2012 . 30 August 2012.
    <http://en.wikipedia.org/wiki/Percutaneous_endoscopic_gastrostomy>.

11. Tresca, Amber J. *About Us.* 21 August 2012. 30 August 2012.
    <http://ibdcrohns.about.com/cs/diagnostictesting/a/colonoscopyprep.htm>.

12. School, Faculty Harvard Medical. *Intelihealth*. 08 December 2010. 30 August 2012.
    <http://intelihealth.com/IH/ihtPrint/WSIHW000/9339/31212.html>.

13. *Farlex, Inc.* 2012. 30 August 2012. <http://medical-dictionary.thefreedictionary.com/cystic+fibrosis>.

14. *Unyts*. 2012. 30 August 2012. <http://unyts.org/>.

15. Manzone, Rick. *Yellow Car...I WIN! The Story of Beans and Roses*. Arcade, NY: Springville Print Shop, 2012.

16. B, Lauren. *Remedy Health Media, LLC*. 25 August 2008. 30 August 2012. <http://www.wellsphere.com/cystic-fibrosis-article/finger-clubbing-in-cystic-fibrosis/213866 >.

17. *Wikimapia*. n.d. 30 August 2012.
    <http://wikimapia.org/5290609/Crile-Building>.

18. *Blogspot*. 15 January 2008. 30 August 2012.
    <http://understandingcysticfibrosis.blogspot.com/2008/01/tune-ups-explained.html>.

DISCLAIMER
This book is my personal experience with cystic fibrosis. It is meant to provide some information and awareness of the illness, but should not be a replacement for any medical guidance. Under no circumstances should my book be held responsible for anything you may do regarding your own health care. The information in this book is believed to be accurate and up to date, but cannot be guaranteed.